D0868237

Praise for the First ~~Edition~~

Businessmen and theologians are like distant cousins, and often they're just not on speaking terms. If anything can bring them into conversation, it's this superb catechism, which achieves the minor miracle of being both erudite and readable.

—*John L. Allen Jr., Associate Editor,* The Boston Globe

Some say that in today's business world, leaders need to check their faith at the door. My own career experience indicates that every day provides the opportunity, with each personal interaction and with every business decision, to draw upon our moral compass formed by our faith. In my view, having *A Catechism for Business* as a ready reference of Catholic teaching regarding business ethics can help the busy executive stay well grounded, and also provide great insight, when dealing with particularly tough ethical issues. I applaud the efforts of Abela and Capizzi to make these important teachings of our faith readily available to business and governmental leaders.

Lawrence J. Blanford, President and CEO,
Green Mountain Coffee Roasters, Inc. (Retired)

A practical *vade mecum* for prompt consultation on fundamental ethical questions, with extensive sources for further reflection.

Camilla Borghese Khevenhüller-Metsch, President and
Managing Director, Istituto Biochimico Italiano

Many of us in business never considered that the Church has much to say about how we operate our companies. In fact, as this book demonstrates, that's not at all true. In Abela and Capizzi's well organized and accessible book, we see clearly how much we were missing. The more we learn about what the social doctrine has to say about business, and the harder we work to apply those precepts in our professional lives, the stronger our companies become! So doing the right thing is also doing the smart thing: how could God arrange it any other way?

William H. Bowman, CEO, The Core
Values Group LLC

Catholic social doctrine has grown into a vast field. This excellent handbook finds its way through a series of key questions and answers, the questions being those that arise naturally in the course of a working day.

This is the most useful book for a Catholic business manager that I have ever seen. It enables the reader to tap directly into the wisdom of the Church's magisterium.

Stratford Caldecott, editor, Second Spring,
Research Fellow, St Benet's Hall, Oxford, and
author, The Radiance of Being

This document is a real service to the business community and will prove to be an essential tool in the toolbox: a businessperson's secret weapon.

Dawn Carpenter, Senior Vice President,
JPMorganChase

A Catechism for Business is an excellent source to reflect, and guide us through the challenging moral decisions that will affect every successful organization. It belongs in your resource library.

Lou DiCerbo, CLU, ChFC, RFC, Chairman
Emeritus, Round Table of New York

Profs. Abela and Capizzi have created a desperately needed resource for the business community. Our society completely neglects the Church's two thousand years of wisdom and guidance, particularly in the area of commerce where board room decisions are reduced to mere economic considerations. This book presents the Church's teaching on many specific areas of consideration in a concise and easily accessible format and is sure to have a much-needed impact on our morally impaired society.

Gellert Dornay, CEO, Axia Home Loans

Abela and Capizzi offer an inspired product: practical business advice based on sound Catholic teaching. *A Catechism for Business* is not a shortcut to success–or to Heaven–but living your faith in your business life is sure to bear fruit, in this life and beyond.

Hon. Mike Ferguson, Member of Congress (2001–2009),
CEO, Ferguson Strategies LLC

By framing Church teaching with a series of questions, Drs. Abela and Capizzi have produced an invaluable reference for Catholics seeking to intertwine their faith and work. Is it morally acceptable to bluff? Can we charge whatever price the market will bear? *A Catechism for Business* presents the relevant Church teaching to these and many other business questions in this well thought out and engaging book.

Sean Fieler, President, Equinox Partners, LP

This book is pure gift to our age. It would not surprise me if it became a handbook for generations to come. It belongs in the briefcase, if not on the desk, of every serious Catholic, and perhaps even every serious Christian, businessman and woman.

Brian Gail, former CEO and bestselling Catholic author

A Catechism for Business reminds us that, even as business leaders, we are standing on the shoulders of giants, participants in a great unfolding story of tradition, teaching and revelation. Dr. Abela and Dr. Capizzi have given us all an immeasurable blessing by compiling the business-specific works of the Church. *A Catechism for Business* will be my companion for years to come. Thank you!

Adam Gardiner, Founder and CVO, AdjusterPro

The increasingly secular focus of the governmental and business communities create ongoing challenges for people of faith. Questions regarding morality, ethics and the consequences of business decisions and policies arise more regularly as outcomes affecting various stakeholders are considered. Drs. Abela and Capizzi and their researchers have unlocked and organized in a clear and concise format, Mother Church's teachings on the most specific questions of business ethics and morality. Finally, a sorely needed reference and guidebook exists for Catholic and business leaders of all faiths who believe that ethically responsible business decisions and successful economic outcomes are not mutually exclusive concepts … an important message at a critical point in time.

Andrew Gatto, former CEO, Russ Berrie and Co.

Written from a Catholic perspective, rooted in profound biblical truths and centuries of Church experience, *A Catechism for Business* is not merely a guide for the Catholic business person, but can well serve all those who share a common desire to study, contemplate and internalize how best to serve humanity, regardless of their religious affiliation.

John Guevremont, Major, USMC (Retired)

Business Ethics is a hot topic, but the substance of what is discussed is usually vague and uninspired. Thankfully Abela and Capizzi, in their *Catechism for Business*, have set a new standard, combining insight, thoroughness, and recourse to the greatest treasury of moral thinking that exists in the world.

Frank Hanna, CEO, Hanna Capital, and author,
What Your Money Means

A Catechism for Business is a valuable guide for business professionals at all levels who inevitably encounter situations that test their ability to navigate the waters of business ethics. I highly recommend this remarkable resource to businessmen and women who wish to grow in synch with the Church's wisdom and authority.

John J. Hunt, Executive Director, Legatus

This book is an invaluable resource for board members of non-profits. It is often the role of the board to counsel senior leadership on thorny issues of organizational direction and management. Basing that counsel on the wisdom of Catholic teaching is literally a Godsend.

J. Patrick Kearns, Chairman, Fulcrum Securities

Business schools frequently teach business ethics with a view that there are no right or wrong answers. Profs. Abela and Capizzi provide quotes from Church teaching to show that in ethics there is a right and wrong answer. This "Catechism" belongs on every executive's credenza—and an extra copy on the nightstand.

James Longon, Owner, HQ Global Workplaces

Finally, a consolidation of the Church's teachings organized in a way to help business leaders leverage the Church's wisdom as we think through the everyday issues we face. This is the most useful book on faith and business that I have ever seen.

Denis McFarlane, CEO, Infinitive

Dean Andrew Abela and Prof. Joe Capizzi allow us to participate in the Papal and Conciliar dialogue that has unfolded over the past century and a half regarding the conduct of Catholics in business and markets, a dialogue that has become all the more immediate given the globalization of the economy, and the ever increasing impact of markets on everyday life.

Michael J. Millette, Partner and Global Head of Structured Finance, Goldman, Sachs & Co.

This is a brilliantly conceived and executed handbook. I imagine that it will be translated into many languages around the world. *A Catechism for Business* is the most practical handbook of Christian social teaching in relation to the vocation of persons in business ever produced.

Michael Novak, 1994 Templeton Laureate

A Catholic businessperson is faced daily with ethical questions regarding the formation, marketing and sale of his or her product. That businessperson may be surprised to learn, as I was, how much assistance can be received from the social teachings of the Church. Drs. Abela and Capizzi have provided a unique and substantial contribution to this discussion in *A Catechism for Business*. Those who remember the *Baltimore Catechism* appreciate how this mode of instruction was so important to us in learning our faith. Here, the authors use the same format to explore the Church's teachings on business ethics. *A Catechism for Business* is, at once, a thoughtful and enlightening "read" and a useful reference book for ethical considerations.

Stephen G. Peroutka, Founding and Managing Partner,
Peroutka and Peroutka, P.A., radio talk show host,
and founder, National Pro Life Radio

Those who study this Catechism attentively may have to rethink how they debate economic issues, and, more importantly, how they do business. They will understand why Catholic social teaching consistently points beyond "the binary logic of market-plus-state" (*Caritas in Veritate*). Professors Abela and Capizzi are to be congratulated for their thorough and responsible selection of texts.

David L. Schindler, Dean Emeritus and Gagnon
Professor of Fundamental Theology, John Paul II Institute,
The Catholic University of America, and author,
Ordering Love: Liberal Societies and the
Memory of God

A tremendous guide for those who want to succeed in business and work ethically along the way, for use by Catholics and non-Catholics alike.

Amy B. Smith, CEO, The Legacy Mission, and
former Vice President, Fortune 500 company

I suspect that many business people lead separate lives, with our faith in one box, and our business challenges in another. Abela and Capizzi's wonderful and authoritative book shows us how to integrate the two.

Russell Sparkes, Chief Investment Officer, Methodist
Church of Britain, and author, Cardinal Manning and
the Birth of Catholic Social Teaching

Rather than the usual interpretations, Andrew Abela and Joe Capizzi offer business decision makers a very useful practical guide to the original documents of Catholic social teaching: on each ethical dilemma, as they arise in real life, they will bring you, not to any simple solution, but to a treasure of suggestions to enrich your own meditation. Perhaps not an easy track, but one which puts you on Pope Francis's steps: "Business is a vocation, and a noble vocation, provided that those engaged in it see themselves challenged by a greater meaning in life" (*Evangelii Gaudium,* November 2013).

Domingo Sugranyes, President, Fondazione
Centesimus Annus Pro Pontifice

In *A Catechism for Business*, Andrew Abela and Joe Capizzi prove that it is possible to be successful in business and stay true to your beliefs. Drawing on Church teachings, this unique book is the perfect checkpoint to make sure you are on track—both in business and in faith. Anyone seeking guidance on how to successfully apply morality and ethics as a business leader will find these keen insights indispensable.

Mark Weber, President, NetApp U.S. Public Sector

Few are aware that Catholic leaders, particularly the popes, have presented profound insights on issues that have direct bearing upon the challenges that business people face today. Up to now, one would have to read thousands of pages of church documents to locate salient nuggets for advice on a particular moral question that a business person or policy maker faces. *A Catechism for Business* fills a critical need in today's complex world, where moral answers to questions are not always clear-cut. This well-organized and concise book is an absolute must for business people and policy makers "in the trenches" as well as for academics, and even theologians, focused on the common good.

Luanne Zurlo, Founder and former President and
Executive Director, WorldFund

A Catechism
for Business

A Catechism *for* Business

Tough Ethical Questions & Insights from Catholic Teaching

Second Edition

Edited by Andrew V. Abela and
Joseph E. Capizzi

THE CATHOLIC UNIVERSITY OF AMERICA PRESS
WASHINGTON, D.C.

Design and typesetting by Kachergis Book Design

Cataloging-in-Publication Data available from
the Library of Congress
ISBN 978-0-8132-2884-6 (pbk. : alk. paper)

Contents

Applicability of Catholic Teaching to Business Issues

Moral Dilemmas in Business

Benefits

Working Conditions

6. International Business 119

7. Particularly Morally Sensitive Industries 125

Health Care

8. Conclusion 143

Introduction to the
Second Edition

If ever proof were needed that Catholic social doctrine is a living and vibrant tradition, the need for a second edition of our *A Catechism for Business: Tough Ethical Questions and Insights from Catholic Teaching* would be that proof. The first, and lesser, reason is the fabulous response to the book. We are overjoyed that so many readers found the book useful. We are pleased that many were moved to contact us. They thanked us for having put the Church's social doctrine together with challenging questions, and they made small recommendations to us for any new editions of the book. The most common suggestion was to remove the few editorial comments that appeared in the first edition. We thank you for that wise advice and have happily complied! But the response to *A Catechism for Business* has been spectacular, and we are convinced this enthusiasm is a positive sign of the role Catholic social doctrine plays in the new evangelization.

The second, and by far most important, reason for a second edition is the need to incorporate the recent pronouncements on Catholic social doctrine issued by Pope Francis. Pope Francis's pontificate has so far been animated by deep concern for the Church's social mission, especially as part of the Church's effort to come to the aid of those in need and as part—an essential part—of evangelization. Pope Francis never tires of reminding the faithful that concern for the poor is built into the evangelical mission of the Church. On July 27, 2013, in a Mass for priests and religious in Rio de Janeiro at World Youth Day, Pope Francis connected evangelization with encounter. And like Popes John Paul II and Benedict before him, he turned to the Virgin Mary as his exemplar of this "evangelization by encounter." He said, "Let us ask her to teach us to encounter one another in Jesus every day. And when we pretend not to notice because we have many things to do and the tabernacle is abandoned, may she take us by the hand. Let us ask this of her! Watch over me, Mother, when I am disoriented, and lead me by the hand. May you spur us on to meet our many brothers and sisters who are on the outskirts, who are hungry for God but have no one to proclaim him." That is the purpose of this book: to help business people of good will encounter one another in Jesus every day.

We dedicate this second edition to the most important mothers in our lives: our mothers, our Mother, and the mothers of our children.

Introduction to the First Edition

The incidence of scandal arising from ethical violations in the business world has been increasing over the past several years. At work, many managers who consider themselves to be faithful are all too willing to "check their religion at the door," often simply because they are unaware of the implications of their faith for their business practices. The purpose of this book is to help change this state of affairs by presenting the teachings of the Catholic Church as they relate to specific questions in business ethics.

Catholic social teaching has been called "the Church's best-kept secret." This is especially true of its applications to business. The Catholic Church over the years has developed extensive guidance of great relevance to many areas of business, but this guidance is often buried within lengthy Church documents not easily accessible to the layperson. When faced with specific ethical questions, Catholics may not know where to search for answers—if they even know that such answers exist. The main contribution of this book is to organize in one volume Church teaching of relevance to business and economics by topic and specific question.

This book does not necessarily set out to offer a definitive answer to each question; business ethics questions are often too complex or subtle for definitive prescriptions to be offered to address all possible situations. The documents composing Catholic social doctrine often remind us that the Church does not claim economic (or business) expertise. Instead she offers principles for reflection to form the consciences of the faithful as they exercise their expertise in the economic realm. The purpose of this book, therefore, is to collect and make accessible Church teaching to facilitate that reflection. We cannot do the interpretation for the reader: only you, in your capacity as a business leader or employee, can apply the teaching to the particular challenges you face. Therefore the book provides the rich insights and useful guidelines from Catholic social doctrine collected into headings and questions based on our experiences with business leaders. We have taken great pains to ensure that we are completely faithful to Church teaching; we provide precise answers where the Church has offered precise answers, and we leave questions open where the Church has left them open. By minimizing commentary and focusing almost exclusively on quotations from magisterial teaching, we have attempted to avoid inserting any biases of our own or others, and instead have tried to let the Church teaching speak for itself directly to you, the reader.

We did include some commentary where we thought it was absolutely essential, but the focus is always on the quotations themselves. That said, we recognize that in the phrasing of the questions, and the selection of responses, and even in the selection of the questions themselves, biases could still have crept in, and we welcome feedback from readers.

The book is organized by major topic (e.g., marketing, finance, manufacturing), sub-topics within those, and then individual questions. After each question, we present the relevant quotations from Church teaching. These quotations are in reverse chronological order, with quotations from the newest documents appearing first, unless one or more of the older quotations are particularly relevant, in which case those are placed first. At times, we have repeated quotations where they are relevant to more than one question.

When you face a moral dilemma in business, we suggest that the best way to use this book is to follow these five steps: (1) find the question that is closest to that dilemma; (2) read the quotations provided; (3) pray and mediate on them; (4) read further in the documents those quotations come from, if necessary; and then (5) apply them to your specific situation.

At times, the quotations may seem to be in tension with each other. Apparent tensions and even contradictions are a challenge to our understanding, and a call to engage more deeply and fully in the teachings of the Church. As you reflect on the quotations, recall that the documents which make up Catholic social doctrine have emerged and developed over a period longer than a century. Most of them were responding to particular social and economic challenges that provoked different emphases than documents coming before or after them. The principles remain the same throughout, though. Thus, for instance, in some documents contemporary challenges like socialism provoked emphatic statements about the natural right to private property, whereas later concerns about excessive materialism and individualism provoked emphatic statements about the right *use* of one's property.

Before we move on to the authority of these documents, allow us to make a few comments about steps 3 and 4. Step 3 asks you to "pray and meditate" on your question and the quotations relevant to it. Step 4 suggests that you read further in the documents from which they come. Together these steps emphasize the need to internalize the teaching, to understand that, though these quotations can be removed from their context to help inform reflection, ultimately Catholic social teaching helps form us as Catholics. We would be disappointed if the model we develop here suggests that living the Catholic life in the business world reduces to the wooden application of some key phrases. The selections of teachings contained here are points of departure, not destinations. They should be used to help begin reflection, a reflection informed by a life of prayerful inquiry. The documents which form Catholic social doctrine appeal to our consciences, as individuals and as members of society. Our consciences, the place where we hear the voice of God, require constant conversation with God as occurs in prayer. Occasionally, the reflective process will require turning to the documents for a fuller understanding of their meaning. Sometimes, urgent and anxiety-producing problems in our work may prove excellent opportunities to deepen our relationship with our Creator.

A Note on Teaching Authority

Readers may wonder why Catholics in business should consult Church teaching, and what exactly is the purpose of such teaching: is it meant to guide business people as they encounter tough moral questions, or is it meant to help one's business succeed? And just what authority does Catholic teaching have in this area? Are we obliged to follow it?

Adhering to Catholic social doctrine in business should not, typically, contradict the pursuit of business success. Understanding this teaching well should help managers see that the longer-term good of their business coincides with the goods of the communities—family, town or city, state, and so on—to which they belong. Being a good Catholic business person means being a good person and being good at business. The two are not opposed. The connection of adhering to and being guided by Catholic social doctrine to being a good person and a successful business person is clearest when we recall that Catholic social doctrine derives from Catholic moral teaching. "Catholic social doctrine" does not mark off some alien body of literature to be imposed onto business or economic life. It is merely a specification of the requirements of the moral life in the context of business and economic matters. Catholic moral teaching aims to guide us to our flourishing; it aims to help us be better, to grow as men and women in our discipleship to Christ and our relationship to the Church. Catholic social doctrine just narrows the scope of that guidance toward our flourishing in the business and economic contexts. To some extent, the term "Catholic social doctrine" can be misleading, suggesting to a greater degree than it should that we've entered something different; that there are "social" and "private" ethics in Catholic moral teaching. Nothing could be further from the truth! All Catholic moral teaching is social: it emerges from a social context (the communion of the Trinity) and aims at the ennobling of all the communities in which men and women find themselves. "Catholic social doctrine" is no more social than teaching on the morality of truth-telling and promise-keeping or any other teaching. All of this moral teaching strives to make us and our communities more faithful, and thereby, more human places to live.

And yet the Church claims no special competence concerning the successful management of a business. Over and over she emphasizes that her teaching is aimed at the human person and the communities of persons. She has no special insight into the operation of businesses. For centuries the Church's moral teachings have affirmed that the moral requirements we have toward each other are not to be followed because someone—that is, the Church—says so, but because we all flourish, in every way, when we follow these teachings. Put simply, employers and employees alike will do better when they treat each other as persons, created in the image and likeness of God. As Pope Leo XIII wrote in his 1891 encyclical *Rerum novarum,* "When Christian morals are completely observed, they yield of themselves a certain measure of prosperity to material existence" (42).

Finally, perhaps the more difficult question concerns the authority of the teaching in this area. Catholics are obliged to follow the moral doctrines of the Church; for instance, Catholic married couples have been instructed by the Church that artificial forms of contraception are always illicit; that is, they do not serve the goods of the spouses in marriage and therefore must be avoided. Is the same true, however, for Church teaching on advertising? How could the Church have something to say to that question remotely similar to what she says regarding contraception?

In partial answer to this we are convinced of two things. First, the Church exists in part to teach us how to attain salvation: this is what we believe as Catholics. We do well, then, to take seriously and prayerfully such advice as she offers in all areas of life. Remember: she is drawing not only on over two thousand years of experience, but also on sacred tradition and scripture. Since 1891, the Church has chosen to speak directly to the world on matters pertaining to business and economics. If she has determined to bring her voice into these areas of life, we would be foolish not to embrace the opportunity to listen and learn. Second, as we hope to make clear, some of what is taught in this area is not merely "business" ethics, but "life" ethics. The moral principles being drawn upon are the same moral principles we encounter in all aspects of life. "You may not do evil that good may come of it," we are taught. This is no less true concerning employee working conditions than it is concerning contraception. We carry into our business our whole selves. We should not be tempted to see our professional lives as separated from our "everyday" lives. To conclude, then, we offer this quotation from Pope Benedict XVI's 2008 address to the U.S. Catholic bishops:

> The subtle influence of secularism can nevertheless color the way people allow their faith to influence their behavior. Is it consistent to profess our beliefs in church on Sunday, and then during the week to promote business practices or medical procedures contrary to those beliefs? Is it consistent for practicing Catholics to ignore or exploit the poor and the marginalized, to promote sexual behavior contrary to Catholic moral teaching, or to adopt positions that contradict the right to life of every human being from conception to natural death? Any tendency to treat religion as a private matter must be resisted. Only when their faith permeates every aspect of their lives do Christians become truly open to the transforming power of the Gospel.

Background, Acknowledgments, and Translations

In May of 2005, during the Legatus Annual Pro-Life Pilgrimage to Washington, D.C., one of the editors of this volume, Andrew Abela, made a presentation about tough ethical questions facing Catholic business executives and insights from Catholic social teaching on these questions. At the end of the presentation, Jim Longon, then president of the Philadelphia

chapter of Legatus, stood up and said, "What you are creating here is a catechism for business." With Jim's support, and
the support of a grant-in-aid distributed under the auspices of
George Garvey, then vice-provost at the Catholic University of
America, we hired two outstanding research assistants, David
Cory and Austin Lipari, both philosophy students at CUA.
Collectively we read through all the documents that make up
the sources for this project, including all the social encyclicals
since Pope Leo XIII's, the *Catechism of the Catholic Church,*
and the relevant documents of Vatican II and the pontifical
councils and congregations, to identify teachings and insights
that are relevant to these tough ethical questions.

The questions themselves dated from an earlier project.
A couple of years before the Legatus presentation, Dr. Abela
was approached by some priests of the order Miles Jesus and
asked to come up with a list of tough ethical questions facing
Catholic business executives, to help them with a project they
were working on for Tom Tracy, a successful entrepreneur. Assured that he would have to provide only the questions and not
the answers, in consultation with several business executives
including many members of Legatus, he created a list of very
tough ethical questions faced in business. Thirty of those questions were answered by William Marshner of Christendom
College, and the questions and answers were published private-
ly. This book expands the scope of that earlier project and seeks
to answer the full list of questions.

Throughout the book our answers draw on quotations from
the documents of the Catholic social tradition and other sources. Unless otherwise specified, all quotations from papal and
conciliar documents are taken from the Vatican's official English
translations, all of which are available at the Vatican website,

www.vatican.va. We identify the quotations by document and paragraph number. For responses coming from the *Catechism of the Catholic Church,* we rely on the official English translation of the second edition (the *editio typica*), published in the United States (United States Catholic Conference-Libreria Editrice Vaticana, 1997). We identify those quotations by paragraph number and page number (in parentheses) in this edition of the book.

We are grateful to the Catholic University of America community, including especially President John Garvey, Provost Jim Brennan, Dean Mark Morozowich of the School of Theology and Religious Studies, and his predecessor, Monsignor Kevin Irwin, and Trevor Lipscombe and Jim Kruggel of the Catholic University of America Press. Finally, our thanks to our spouses and children for their patience and support during the completion of this book. We dedicate this book to St. Joseph, patron saint of workers.

A
Catechism
for Business

—1—

General Questions

Economic Context

1. Do we have a right to private property?

"In the beginning God entrusted the earth and its resources to the common stewardship of mankind to take care of them, master them by labor, and enjoy their fruits. [footnote reference to Gn 1:26–29] The goods of creation are destined for the whole human race. However, the earth is divided up among men to assure the security of their lives, endangered by poverty and threatened by violence. The appropriation of property is legitimate for guaranteeing the freedom and dignity of persons and for helping each of them to meet his basic needs and the needs of those in his charge."

—*Catechism of the Catholic Church*, 2402 (577)

"The private ownership of goods is justified by the need to protect and increase them, so that they can better serve the common good."

—Francis, *Evangelii Gaudium*, 189

"The Christian tradition has never recognized the right to private property as absolute or inviolable, and has stressed the social purpose of all forms of private property."

—Francis, *Laudato Si*, 93

"[The right to private property,] which is fundamental for the autonomy and development of the person, has always been defended by the Church up to our own day. At the same time, the Church teaches that the possession of material goods is not an absolute right, and that its limits are inscribed in its very nature as a human right."

—St. John Paul II, *Centesimus annus*, 30

"[The principle of private property] as it was then stated and as it is still taught by the Church, *diverges* radically from the program of *collectivism* as proclaimed by Marxism and put into practice in various countries in the decades following the time of Leo XIII's Encyclical. At the same time it differs from the program of *capitalism* practiced by liberalism and by the political systems inspired by it. In the latter case, the difference consists in the way the right to ownership or property is understood. Christian tradition has never upheld this right as absolute and untouchable. On the contrary, it has always understood this right within the broader context of the right common to all to use the goods of the whole of creation: *the right to private property is subordinated to the right to common use*, to the fact that goods are meant for everyone."

—St. John Paul II, *Laborem exercens*, 14

"Private property or some ownership of external goods confers on everyone a sphere wholly necessary for the autonomy of the person and the family, and it should be regarded as an extension of human freedom."

—*Gaudium et spes,* 71

"Let it be considered as certain and established that neither [Pope Leo XIII] nor those theologians who have taught under the guidance and authority of the Church have ever denied or questioned the twofold character of ownership, called usually individual or social according as it regards either separate persons or the common good. For they have always unanimously maintained that nature, rather the Creator Himself, has given man the right of private ownership not only that individuals may be able to provide for themselves and their families but also that the goods which the Creator destined for the entire family of mankind may through this institution truly serve this purpose. All this can be achieved in no wise except through the maintenance of a certain and definite order."

—Pius XI, *Quadragesimo anno,* 45

"For, every man has by nature the right to possess property as his own."

—Leo XIII, *Rerum novarum,* 6

2. How should each person use his or her private property?

'The principle of the subordination of private property to the universal destination of goods, and thus the right of everyone to their use, is a golden rule of social conduct and "the first principle of the whole ethical and social order."'

—Francis, *Laudato Si,* 93 (quoting St. John Paul II, *Laborem Exercens,* 19)

"'But if the question be asked, how must one's possessions be used? the Church replies without hesitation that man should not consider his material possessions as his own, but as common to all...,' because 'above the laws and judgments of men stands the law, the judgment of Christ.'"

—St. John Paul II, *Centesimus annus,* 30 (quoting Leo XIII, *Rerum novarum,* 22, in turn quoting St. Thomas Aquinas, *Summa theologiae,* II–II, q. 66, resp. to a. 2)

"Telling the Parable of the dishonest but very crafty administrator, Christ teaches his disciples the best way to use money and material riches, that is, to share them with the poor, thus acquiring their friendship, with a view to the Kingdom of Heaven. 'Make friends for yourselves by means of unrighteous mammon,' Jesus says, 'so that when it fails they may receive you into the eternal habitations' (Lk 16:9)....Here one could open up a vast and complex field of reflection on the theme of poverty and riches, also on a world scale, in which two logics of economics oppose each other: the logic of profit and that of the equal distribution of goods, which do not contradict each other if their relationship is well ordered. Catholic social doctrine has always supported that equitable distribution of goods is a priority. Naturally, profit is legitimate and, in just measure, necessary for economic development."

—Benedict XVI, Angelus (September 23, 2007)

"Money is not 'dishonest' in itself, but more than anything else it can close man in a blind egocentrism. It therefore concerns a type of work of 'conversion' of economic goods: instead of using them only for self-interest, it is also necessary to think of the needs of the poor, imitating Christ himself, who, as St. Paul wrote: 'though he was rich, yet for your sake he became poor, so that by his poverty you might become rich' (2 Cor 8:9)."

—Benedict XVI, Angelus (September 23, 2007)

"God gave the earth to the whole human race for the sustenance of all its members, without excluding or favoring anyone. This is *the foundation of the universal destination of the earth's goods.*"

—St. John Paul II, *Centesimus annus*, 31

"The basis for the social doctrine of the Church is the principle of *the universal destination of goods.* According to the plan of God the goods of the earth are offered to all people and to each individual as a means towards the development of a truly human life. At the service of this destination of goods is *private property*, which—precisely for this purpose—possesses an *intrinsic social function.*"

—St. John Paul II, *Christifideles laici*, 43

"Individual persons may not use their resources without considering the effects that this use will have, rather they must act in a way that benefits not only themselves and their family but also the common good. From this there arises the duty on the part of owners not to let the goods in their possession go idle and to channel them to productive activity, even entrusting them to others who are desirous and capable of putting them to use in production."

—Pontifical Council for Justice and Peace, *Compendium of the Social Doctrine of the Church*, 178

"No one may appropriate surplus goods solely for his own private use when others lack the bare necessities of life. In short, 'as the Fathers of the Church and other eminent theologians tell us, the right of private property may never be exercised to the detriment of the common good.'"

—Paul VI, *Populorum progressio*, 23 (quoting letter to the fifty-second Social Week at Brest, in *L'homme et la révolution urbaine*, Lyon: Chronique sociale 1965: 8–9)

"We should notice at this point that the right of private owner-ship is clearly sanctioned by the Gospel. Yet at the same time, the divine Master frequently extends to the rich the insistent invitation to convert their material goods into spiritual ones by conferring them on the poor. 'Lay not up to yourselves trea-sures on earth; where the rust and moth consume and where thieves break through and steal. But lay up to yourselves trea-sures in heaven; where neither the rust nor moth doth con-sume, and where thieves do not break through nor steal.' And the Lord will look upon the charity given to the poor as given to Himself. 'Amen, I say to you, as long as you did it to one of these my least brethren, you did it to me.'"

—St. John XXIII, *Mater et magistra,* 121

"Furthermore, a person's superfluous income, that is, income which he does not need to sustain life fittingly and with digni-ty, is not left wholly to his own free determination. Rather the Sacred Scriptures and the Fathers of the Church constantly declare in the most explicit language that the rich are bound by a very grave precept to practice almsgiving, beneficence, and munificence.

"Expending larger incomes so that opportunity for gainful work may be abundant, provided, however, that this work is applied to producing really useful goods, ought to be consid-ered...an outstanding exemplification of the virtue of munif-icence and one particularly suited to the needs of the times."

—Pius XI, *Quadragesimo anno,* 50–51

"No one, certainly, is obliged to assist others out of what is re-quired for his own necessary use or for that of his family, or even to give to others what he himself needs to maintain his station in life becomingly and decently....But when the demands of necessity and propriety have been sufficiently met, it is a duty to give to the poor out of that which remains."

—Leo XIII, *Rerum novarum*, 36

3. Does the state have a role in facilitating the universal destination of goods?

"Helping the poor financially must always be a provisional solution in the face of pressing needs. The broader objective should always be to allow them a dignified life through work."

—Francis, *Laudato Si*, 128

"The State which would provide everything, absorbing everything into itself, would ultimately become a mere bureaucracy incapable of guaranteeing the very thing which the suffering person—every person—needs: namely, loving personal concern. We do not need a State which regulates and controls everything, but a State which, in accordance with the principle of subsidiarity, generously acknowledges and supports initiatives arising from the different social forces and combines spontaneity with closeness to those in need."

—Benedict XVI, *Deus caritas est*, 28

"[Ownership reform] cannot be achieved by an *a priori elimination of private ownership of the means of production.* For it must be noted that merely taking these means of production (capital) out of the hands of their private owners is not enough to ensure their satisfactory socialization. They cease to be the property of a certain social group, namely the private owners, and become the property of organized society, coming under the administration and direct control of another group of people, namely those who, though not owning them, from the fact of exercising power in society *manage* them on the level of the whole national or the local economy."

—St. John Paul II, *Laborem exercens*, 14

"When the State brings private ownership into harmony with the needs of the common good, it does not commit a hostile act against private owners but rather does them a friendly service; for it thereby effectively prevents the private possession of goods, which the Author of nature in His most wise providence ordained for the support of human life, from causing intolerable evils and thus rushing to its own destruction; it does not destroy private possessions, but safeguards them; and it does not weaken private property rights, but strengthens them."

—Pius XI, *Quadragesimo anno*, 49

"[The benefits of private property], however, can be reckoned on only provided that a man's means be not drained and exhausted by excessive taxation. The right to possess private property is derived from nature, not from man; and the State has the right to control its use in the interests of the public good alone, but by no means to absorb it altogether. The State would therefore be unjust and cruel if under the name of taxation it were to deprive the private owner of more than is fair."

—Leo XIII, *Rerum novarum*, 47

4. Does the Catholic Church recommend any specific economic model (e.g., capitalism, socialism)?

"The Church has no models to present; models that are real and truly effective can only arise within the framework of different historical situations, through the efforts of all those who responsibly confront concrete problems in all their social, economic, political and cultural aspects, as these interact with one another."

—St. John Paul II, *Centesimus annus,* 43

5. Is Catholic social teaching on economics some sort of middle or third way between capitalism and socialism?

"The Church's social doctrine is not a 'third way' between liberal capitalism and Marxist collectivism.... It constitutes a category of its own...[as] the accurate formulation of the results of a careful reflection on the complex realities of human existence...in the light of faith and of the Church's tradition. Its main aim is to interpret these realities, determining their conformity with or divergence from the lines of the Gospel teaching on man and his vocation...to guide Christian behavior."

—St. John Paul II, *Sollicitudo rei socialis,* 41

6. Does socialism fit with Catholic teaching?

"Solidarity is first and foremost a sense of responsibility on the part of everyone with regard to everyone, and it cannot therefore be merely delegated to the State."

—Benedict XVI, *Caritas in veritate,* 38

"The illusion that a policy of mere redistribution of existing wealth can definitively resolve the problem must be set aside. In a modern economy, the value of assets is utterly dependent on the capacity to generate revenue in the present and the future. Wealth creation therefore becomes an inescapable duty, which must be kept in mind if the fight against material poverty is to be effective in the long term."

—Benedict XVI, message for World Day of Peace 2009, 11

"The historical experience of socialist countries has sadly demonstrated that collectivism does not do away with alienation but rather increases it, adding to it a lack of basic necessities and economic inefficiency."

—St. John Paul II, *Centesimus annus*, 41

"By intervening directly and depriving society of its responsibility, the Social Assistance State leads to a loss of human energies and an inordinate increase of public agencies, which are dominated more by bureaucratic ways of thinking than by concern for serving their clients, and which are accompanied by an enormous increase in spending."

—St. John Paul II, *Centesimus annus*, 48

"Experience shows us that the denial of this right [of economic initiative], or its limitation in the name of an alleged 'equality' of everyone in society, diminishes, or in practice absolutely destroys, the spirit of initiative, that is to say the creative subjectivity of the citizen. As a consequence, there arises, not so much a true equality as a 'leveling down.'"

—St. John Paul II, *Sollicitudo rei socialis*, 15

"If Socialism, like all errors, contains some truth ..., it is based nevertheless on a theory of human society peculiar to itself and irreconcilable with true Christianity. Religious socialism, Christian socialism, are contradictory terms; no one can be at the same time a good Catholic and a true socialist."

—Pius XI, *Quadragesimo anno*, 120

7. Does capitalism fit with Catholic teaching?

"If by 'capitalism' is meant an economic system which recognizes the fundamental and positive role of business, the market, private property and the resulting responsibility for the means

of production, as well as free human creativity in the economic sector, then the answer is certainly in the affirmative, even
though it would perhaps be more appropriate to speak of a
'business economy', 'market economy' or simply 'free economy'.
But if by 'capitalism' is meant a system in which freedom in
the economic sector is not circumscribed within a strong juridical framework which places it at the service of human freedom in its totality, and which sees it as a particular aspect of
that freedom, the core of which is ethical and religious, then
the reply is certainly negative."

—St. John Paul II, *Centesimus annus*, 42

"While the earnings of a minority are growing exponentially,
so too is the gap separating the majority from the prosperity
enjoyed by those happy few. This imbalance is the result of
ideologies which defend the absolute autonomy of the marketplace and financial speculation. Consequently, they reject
the right of states, charged with vigilance for the common
good, to exercise any form of control."

—Francis, *Evangelii Gaudium*, 56

"Economic freedom is only one element of human freedom.
When it becomes autonomous, when man is seen more as a
producer or consumer of goods than as a subject who produces and consumes in order to live, then economic freedom loses
its necessary relationship to the human person and ends up by
alienating and oppressing him."

—St. John Paul II, *Centesimus annus*, 39

"The ultimate consequences of the individualist spirit in economic life are those which you yourselves, Venerable Brethren
and Beloved Children, see and deplore: Free competition has
destroyed itself; economic dictatorship has supplanted the

free market; unbridled ambition for power has likewise succeeded greed for gain; all economic life has become tragically hard, inexorable, and cruel. To these are to be added the grave evils that have resulted from an intermingling and shameful confusion of the functions and duties of public authority with those of the economic sphere—such as, one of the worst, the virtual degradation of the majesty of the State, which although it ought to sit on high like a queen and supreme arbitress, free from all partiality and intent upon the one common good and justice, is become a slave, surrendered and delivered to the passions and greed of men."

—Pius XI, *Quadragesimo Anno*, 109

8. What is the role of the state in the economy, and how should it perform this role?

"It is the responsibility of the State to safeguard and promote the common good of society"

—Francis, *Evangelii Gaudium*, 240

"The State...has the task of determining the juridical framework within which economic affairs are to be conducted, and thus of safeguarding the prerequisites of a free economy, which presumes a certain equality between the parties, such that one party would not be so powerful as practically to reduce the other to subservience."

—St. John Paul II, *Centesimus annus*, 15

"When both the logic of the market and the logic of the State come to an agreement that each will continue to exercise a monopoly over its respective area of influence, in the long term much is lost: solidarity in relations between citizens, participation and adherence, actions of gratuitousness, all of which stand in contrast with *giving in order to acquire* (the logic of exchange) and *giving through duty* (the logic of public obligation, imposed by State law). In order to defeat underdevelopment, action is required not only on improving exchange-based transactions and implanting public welfare structures, but above all on gradually *increasing openness, in a world context, to forms of economic activity marked by* [a due measure] *of gratuitousness and communion.* The exclusively binary model of market-plus-State is corrosive of society, while economic forms based on solidarity, which find their natural home in civil society without being restricted to it, build up society....Both the market and politics need individuals who are open to reciprocal gift."

—Benedict XVI, *Caritas in veritate*, 39

9. What is the principle of subsidiarity, and what are its implications for the role of the State?

"Let us keep in mind the principle of subsidiarity, which grants freedom to develop the capabilities present at every level of society, while also demanding a greater sense of responsibility for the common good from those who wield greater power."

—Francis, *Laudato Si*, 196

"Subsidiarity respects personal dignity by recognizing in the person a subject who is always capable of giving something to others. By considering reciprocity as the heart of what it is to be a human being, subsidiarity is the most effective antidote against any form of all-encompassing welfare state."

—Benedict XVI, *Caritas in veritate*, 57

"Subsidiarity—insofar as it encourages men and women to enter freely into life-giving relationships with those to whom they are most closely connected and upon whom they most immediately depend, and demands of higher authorities respect for these relationships—manifests a 'vertical' dimension pointing towards the Creator of the social order (cf. Rom 12:16, 18). A society that honors the principle of subsidiarity liberates people from a sense of despondency and hopelessness, granting them the freedom to engage with one another in the spheres of commerce, politics and culture (cf. *Quadragesimo Anno,* 80). When those responsible for the public good attune themselves to the natural human desire for self-governance based on subsidiarity, they leave space for individual responsibility and initiative, but most importantly, they leave space for love (cf. Rom 13:8; *Deus Caritas Est,* 28), which always remains 'the most excellent way' (cf. 1 Cor 12:31)."

—Benedict XVI, address to participants in the fourteenth session of the Pontifical Academy of Social Sciences (May 3, 2008)

"The State must contribute to the achievement of... [unemployment support, adequate wage levels, humane working conditions] both directly and indirectly. Indirectly and according to the *principle of subsidiarity,* by creating favorable conditions for the free exercise of economic activity.... Directly and according to the *principle of solidarity,* by defending the weakest, by placing certain limits on the autonomy of the parties who determine working conditions, and by ensuring in every case the necessary minimum support for the unemployed worker."

—St. John Paul II, *Centesimus annus,* 15

"[The principle of subsidiarity states that] just as it is gravely wrong to take from individuals what they can accomplish by their own initiative and industry and give it to the com-

munity, so also it is an injustice and at the same time a grave
evil and disturbance of right order to assign to a greater and
higher association what lesser and subordinate organizations
can do."

—Pius XI, *Quadragesimo anno*, 79

"The supreme authority of the State ought, therefore, to let
subordinate groups handle matters and concerns of lesser importance, which would otherwise dissipate its efforts greatly.
Thereby the State will more freely, powerfully, and effectively
do all those things that belong to it alone because it alone can
do them: directing, watching, urging, restraining, as occasion
requires and necessity demands. Therefore, those in power should be sure that the more perfectly a graduated order
is kept among the various associations, in observance of the
principle of "subsidiary function," the stronger social authority
and effectiveness will be the happier and more prosperous the
condition of the State."

—Pius XI, *Quadragesimo anno*, 80

10. Is the State responsible for enforcing the principle of
subsidiarity *within* the economy?

"Civil authorities have the right and duty to adopt clear and
firm measures in support of small producers and differentiated
production. To ensure economic freedom from which all can
effectively benefit, restraints occasionally have to be imposed
on those possessing greater resources and financial power. To
claim economic freedom while real conditions bar many people from actual access to it, and while possibilities for employment continue to shrink, is to practice a doublespeak which
brings politics into disrepute."

—Francis, *Laudato Si*, 129

"Saving banks at any cost, making the public pay the price, foregoing a firm commitment to reviewing and reforming the entire system, only reaffirms the absolute power of a financial system, a power which has no future and will only give rise to new crises after a slow, costly and only apparent recovery."

—Francis, *Laudato Si*, 189

11. Can unjust economic structures actually lead people to sin?

"If every action has its consequences, an evil embedded in the structures of a society has a constant potential for disintegration and death. It is evil crystallized in unjust social structures, which cannot be the basis of hope for a better future."

—Francis, *Evangelii Gaudium*, 59

"The decisions which create a human environment can give rise to specific structures of sin which impede the full realization of those who are in any way oppressed by them."

—St. John Paul II, *Centesimus annus*, 38

"[Structures of sin] are rooted in personal sin, and thus always linked to the concrete acts of individuals who introduce these structures, consolidate them and make them difficult to remove. And thus they grow stronger, spread, and become the source of other sins, and so influence people's behavior."

—St. John Paul II, *Sollicitudo rei socialis*, 36

12. How do we overcome unjust economic structures?

"'Structures of sin' are only conquered—presupposing the help of divine grace—by a diametrically opposed attitude: a commitment to the good of one's neighbor with the readiness, in the gospel sense, to 'lose oneself' for the sake of the other instead of exploiting him, and to 'serve him' instead of oppressing him for one's own advantage."

—St. John Paul II, *Sollicitudo rei socialis*, 38

13. Is reforming unjust economic structures sufficient to achieve economic justice?

"There are no just structures without people who want to be just."

—*Catechism of the Catholic Church*, 2832 (680)

"Changing structures without generating new convictions and attitudes will only ensure that those same structures will become, sooner or later, corrupt, oppressive and ineffectual."

—Francis, *Evangelii Gaudium*, 189

"The Church is of course aware of the complexity of the problems confronting society and of the difficulties in finding adequate solutions to them. Nevertheless she considers that the first thing to be done is to appeal to the spiritual and moral capacities of the individual and to the permanent need for inner conversion, if one is to achieve the economic and social changes that will truly be at the service of man. . . . It remains true however that structures established for people's good are of themselves incapable of securing and guaranteeing that good. The corruption which in certain countries affects the leaders and the state of bureaucracy, and which destroys all honest social life, is a proof of this. Moral integrity is a necessary condition for the health of society. It is therefore necessary to work simultaneously for the conversion of hearts and for the improvement of structures."

—Cardinal Joseph Ratzinger, *Libertatis Conscientia*, Instruction on Christian Freedom and Liberation, 75

"[Karl Marx] forgot that man always remains man. He forgot man and he forgot man's freedom. He forgot that freedom always remains also freedom for evil. He thought that once the economy had been put right, everything would automatically be put right. His real error is materialism: man, in fact, is not merely the product of economic conditions, and it is not possible to redeem him purely from the outside by creating a favorable economic environment."

—Benedict XVI, *Spe salvi*, 21

"We must ask ourselves: what does 'progress' really mean; what does it promise and what does it not promise? In the nineteenth century, faith in progress was already subject to critique. In the twentieth century, Theodor W. Adorno formulated the problem of faith in progress quite drastically: he said that progress, seen accurately, is progress from the sling to the atom bomb. Now this is certainly an aspect of progress that must not be concealed. To put it another way: the ambiguity of progress becomes evident. Without doubt, it offers new possibilities for good, but it also opens up appalling possibilities for evil—possibilities that formerly did not exist. We have all witnessed the way in which progress, in the wrong hands, can become and has indeed become a terrifying progress in evil. If technical progress is not matched by corresponding progress in man's ethical formation, in man's inner growth (cf. Eph 3:16; 2 Cor 4:16), then it is not progress at all, but a threat for man and for the world."

—Benedict XVI, *Spe salvi*, 22

"We confess that the Kingdom of God begun here below in the Church of Christ is not of this world whose form is passing, and that its proper growth cannot be confounded with the progress of civilization, of science or of human technology, but that it consists in an ever more profound knowledge of the unfathomable riches of Christ, an ever stronger hope in eternal blessings, an ever more ardent response to the love of God, and an ever more generous bestowal of grace and holiness among men. But it is this same love which induces the Church to concern herself constantly about the true temporal welfare of men. Without ceasing to recall to her children that they have not here a lasting dwelling, she also urges them to contribute, each according to his vocation and his means, to the welfare of their earthly city, to promote justice, peace and brotherhood among men, to give their aid freely to their brothers, especially to the poorest and most unfortunate. The deep solicitude of the Church, the Spouse of Christ, for the needs of men, for their joys and hopes, their griefs and efforts, is therefore nothing other than her great desire to be present to them, in order to illuminate them with the light of Christ and to gather them all in Him, their only Savior. This solicitude can never mean that the Church conform herself to the things of this world, or that she lessen the ardor of her expectation of her Lord and of the eternal Kingdom."

—Paul VI, *Solemni hac liturgia*, 27

"All experts in social problems are seeking eagerly a structure so fashioned in accordance with the norms of reason that it can lead economic life back to sound and right order. But this order, which We Ourselves ardently long for and with all Our efforts promote, will be wholly defective and incomplete unless all the activities of men harmoniously unite to imitate and attain, in so far as it lies within human strength, the marvelous unity of the Divine plan. We mean that perfect order which the Church with great force and power preaches and which right human reason itself demands, that all things be directed to God as the first and supreme end of all created activity, and that all created good under God be considered as mere instruments to be used only in so far as they conduce to the attainment of the supreme end."

—Pius XI, *Quadragesimo anno*, 136

14. Is the Church in favor of globalization?

"To sustain a lifestyle which excludes others, or to sustain enthusiasm for that selfish ideal, a globalization of indifference has developed. Almost without being aware of it, we end up being incapable of feeling compassion at the outcry of the poor, weeping for other people's pain, and feeling a need to help them, as though all this were someone else's responsibility and not our own. The culture of prosperity deadens us; we are thrilled if the market offers us something new to purchase. In the meantime all those lives stunted for lack of opportunity seem a mere spectacle; they fail to move us."

—Francis, *Evangelii Gaudium*, 54

"Despite some of its structural elements, which should neither be denied nor exaggerated, 'globalization, *a priori*, is neither good nor bad. It will be what people make of it.' We should not be its victims, but rather its protagonists, acting in the light of reason, guided by charity and truth.... The transition inherent in the process of globalization presents great difficulties and dangers that can only be overcome if we are able to appropriate the underlying anthropological and ethical spirit that drives globalization towards the humanizing goal of solidarity. Unfortunately this spirit is often overwhelmed or suppressed by ethical and cultural considerations of an individualistic and utilitarian nature. Globalization is a multifaceted and complex phenomenon which must be grasped in the diversity and unity of all its different dimensions, including the theological dimension. In this way it will be possible to experience and to *steer the globalization of humanity in relational terms, in terms of communion and the sharing of goods.*"

—Benedict XVI, *Caritas in veritate*, 42

"On the other hand—and here we see one of the challenging yet also positive sides of the process of globalization—we now have at our disposal numerous means for offering humanitarian assistance to our brothers and sisters in need, not least modern systems of distributing food and clothing, and of providing housing and care. Concern for our neighbor transcends the confines of national communities and has increasingly broadened its horizon to the whole world."

—Benedict XVI, *Deus caritas est*, 30

"Today's world experiences the phenomenon of globalization as a network of relationships extending over the whole planet. Although from certain points of view this benefits the great family of humanity, and is a sign of its profound aspiration towards unity, nevertheless it also undoubtedly brings with it the risk of vast monopolies and of treating profit as the supreme value. As in all areas of human activity, globalization too must be led by ethics, placing everything at the service of the human person, created in the image and likeness of God."

—Benedict XVI, address to the inaugural session of the Fifth General Conference of the Bishops of Latin America and the Caribbean (May 13, 2007), 2

"Among the important ethical issues facing the business community at present are those associated with the impact of global marketing and advertising on the cultures and values of various countries and people. A sound globalization, carried out in respect for the values of different nations and ethnic groupings, can contribute significantly to the unity of the human family and enable forms of cooperation which are not only economic but also social and cultural. Globalization must become more than simply another name for the absolute relativization of values and the homogenization of life styles and cultures. For this to happen, Christian leaders, also in the commercial sphere, are challenged to bear witness to the liberating and transforming power of Christian truth, which inspires us to place all our talents, our intellectual resources, our persuasive abilities, our experience and our skills at the service of God, our neighbor and the common good of the human family."

—St. John Paul II, message to participants in the conference "The Business
Executive: Social Responsibility and Globalization" (March 3, 2004)

"[Globalization] is a new phenomenon, which needs to be recognized and evaluated with careful and precise study, since it seems clearly 'ambivalent.' It can be something good for man and for society, but could also prove harmful, with serious consequences. Everything depends on certain basic decisions: whether 'globalization' serves man, every individual, or exclusively benefits a development that is not governed by the principles of solidarity, participation or responsible subsidiarity."

—St. John Paul II, address to business and trade-union leaders, "Ethical
Dimension of the Global Economy" (May 2, 2000)

"The ethical implications [of globalization] can be positive or negative. There is an economic globalization which brings some positive consequences, such as efficiency and increased production and which, with the development of economic links between the different countries, can help to bring greater unity among peoples and make possible a better service to the human family. However, if globalization is ruled merely by the laws of the market applied to suit the powerful, the consequences cannot but be negative. These are, for example, the absolutizing of the economy, unemployment, the reduction and deterioration of public services, the destruction of the environment and natural resources, the growing distance between rich and poor, unfair competition which puts the poor nations in a situation of ever increasing inferiority. While acknowledging the positive values which come with globalization, the Church considers with concern the negative aspects which follow in its wake."

—St. John Paul II, *Ecclesia in America*, 20

"The globalized economy must be analyzed in the light of the principles of social justice, respecting the preferential option for the poor who must be allowed to take their place in such an economy, and the requirements of the international common good."

—St. John Paul II, *Ecclesia in America*, 55

"The Church in America is called not only to promote greater integration between nations, thus helping to create an authentic globalized culture of solidarity, but also to cooperate with every legitimate means in reducing the negative effects of globalization, such as the domination of the powerful over the weak, especially in the economic sphere, and the loss of the values of local cultures in favor of a misconstrued homogenization."

—St. John Paul II, *Ecclesia in America*, 55

"As everyone is well aware, there are some countries where there is an imbalance between the amount of arable land and the number of inhabitants; others where there is an imbalance between the richness of the resources and the instruments of agriculture available. It is imperative, therefore, that nations enter into collaboration with each other, and facilitate the circulation of goods, capital and manpower.

"We advocate in such cases the policy of bringing the work to the workers, wherever possible, rather than bringing workers to the scene of the work. In this way many people will be afforded an opportunity of increasing their resources without being exposed to the painful necessity of uprooting themselves from their own homes, settling in a strange environment, and forming new social contacts."

—St. John XXIII, *Pacem in terris*, 101–2

Applicability of Catholic Teaching to Business Issues

15. Is there a spiritual significance to work?

"… the question arises as to the meaning and purpose of all human activity. This has to do not only with manual or agricultural labor but with any activity involving a modification of existing reality, from producing a social report to the design of a technological development. Underlying every form of work is a concept of the relationship which we can and must have with what is other than ourselves."

—Francis, *Laudato Si*, 125

"The problem is not always an excess of activity, but rather activity undertaken badly, without adequate motivation, without a spirituality which would permeate it and make it pleasurable. As a result, work becomes more tiring than necessary, even leading at times to illness."

—Francis, *Evangelii Gaudium*, 82

"Work is of fundamental importance to the fulfillment of the human being and to the development of society. Thus, it must always be organized and carried out with full respect for human dignity and must always serve the common good. At the same time, it is indispensable that people not allow themselves to be enslaved by work or to idolize it, claiming to find in it the ultimate and definitive meaning of life."

—Benedict XVI, post-synodal apostolic exhortation *Sacramentum caritatis*, 74

"The vocation of the businessperson is a genuine human and Christian calling. Its importance in the life of the Church and in the world economy can hardly be overstated."

—Pontifical Council for Justice and Peace, *Vocation of the Business Leader*, 6

"Building a productive organization is a primary way in which businesspeople can share in the unfolding of the work of creation. When they realize that they are participating in the work of the Creator through their stewardship of productive organizations, they may begin to realize the grandeur and awesome responsibility of their vocation."

—Pontifical Council for Justice and Peace, *Vocation of the Business Leader*, 8

"Entrepreneurs, managers, and all who work in business should be encouraged to recognize their work as a true vocation and to respond to God's call in the spirit of true disciples. In doing so, they engage in the noble task of serving their brothers and sisters and of building up the Kingdom of God."

—Pontifical Council for Justice and Peace, *Vocation of the Business Leader*, 87

"Through work man must earn his daily bread and contribute to the continual advance of science and technology and, above all, to elevating unceasingly the cultural and moral level of the society within which he lives in community with those who belong to the same family.... Man is made to be in the visible universe an image and likeness of God himself, and he is placed in it in order to subdue the earth. From the beginning therefore he is *called to work*."

—St. John Paul II, *Laborem exercens,* introduction

"For man, created to God's image, received a mandate to subject to himself the earth and all it contains, and to govern the world with justice and holiness....

"This mandate concerns the whole of everyday activity as well. For while providing the substance of life for themselves and their families, men and women are performing their activities in a way which appropriately benefits society. They can justly consider that by their labor they are unfolding the Creator's work, consulting the advantages of their brother men, and are contributing by their personal industry to the realization in history of the divine plan."

—*Gaudium et spes,* 34

"Professional labor is for Christians a way of serving God. ...Even if, with the years, professional labor should become monotonous, or if, by obedience to the law of God, it should weigh as a constraint, or as a too heavy burden, it should nonetheless always remain for you, Christians, one of the most important means of sanctification, one of the most effective ways of being conformed to the divine will and meriting heaven."

—Pius XII, address to personnel of the Bank of Italy (April 25, 1950)

16. Is Catholic teaching relevant to business management?

"It is no longer possible to claim that religion should be restricted to the private sphere and that it exists only to prepare souls for heaven. We know that God wants his children to be happy in this world too, even though they are called to fulfilment in eternity, for he has created all things "for our enjoyment" (1 Tim 6:17), the enjoyment of everyone."

—Francis, *Evangelii Gaudium*, 182

"... no one can demand that religion should be relegated to the inner sanctum of personal life, without influence on societal and national life, without concern for the soundness of civil institutions, without a right to offer an opinion on events affecting society. Who would claim to lock up in a church and silence the message of Saint Francis of Assisi or Blessed Teresa of Calcutta? They themselves would have found this unacceptable. An authentic faith—which is never comfortable or completely personal—always involves a deep desire to change the world, to transmit values, to leave this earth somehow better than we found it."

—Francis, *Evangelii Gaudium*, 183

"The subtle influence of secularism can nevertheless color the way people allow their faith to influence their behavior. Is it consistent to profess our beliefs in church on Sunday, and then during the week to promote business practices or medical procedures contrary to those beliefs? Is it consistent for practicing Catholics to ignore or exploit the poor and the marginalized, to promote sexual behavior contrary to Catholic moral teaching, or to adopt positions that contradict the right to life of every human being from conception to natural death? Any tendency to treat religion as a private matter must be resisted. Only when their faith permeates every aspect of their lives do Christians become truly open to the transforming power of the Gospel."

—Benedict XVI, address to the bishops of the United States (April 16, 2008)

"The substantial novelty brought by Jesus is that he opened the way to a more human and freer world, with full respect for the distinction and autonomy that exists between what belongs to Caesar and what belongs to God (cf. Mt 22:21). If, therefore, on the one hand, the Church recognizes that she is not and does not intend to be a political agent, on the other, she cannot avoid concerning herself with the good of the whole civil community in which she lives and works and to which she makes her own special contribution, shaping in the political and entrepreneurial classes a genuine spirit of truth and honesty geared to seeking the common good rather than personal advantage."

—Benedict XVI, letter to the president of the Italian Bishops' Conference on the occasion of the centenary of the Italian Catholic Social Week (October 12, 2007)

"Dividing the demands of one's faith from one's work in business is a fundamental error which contributes to much of the damage done by businesses in our world today, including overwork to the detriment of family or spiritual life, an unhealthy attachment to power to the detriment of one's own good, and the abuse of economic power in order to make even greater economic gains."

—Pontifical Council for Justice and Peace, *Vocation of the Business Leader*, 10

"For such a task [developing just economic arrangements] the Church offers her social teaching as an *indispensable and ideal orientation,* a teaching which, as already mentioned, recognizes the positive value of the market and of enterprise, but which at the same time points out that these need to be oriented towards the common good."

—St. John Paul II, *Centesimus annus,* 43

"The Church remains deeply conscious of her 'duty in every age of examining the signs of the times and interpreting them in the light of the Gospel, so that she can offer in a manner appropriate to each generation replies to the continual human questionings on the meaning of this life and the life to come and on how they are related' (*Gaudium et spes,* 4)."

—St. John Paul II, *Veritatis splendor,* 2

"This split between the faith which many profess and their daily lives deserves to be counted among the more serious errors of our age."

—*Gaudium et spes,* 43

17. Will following Church teaching lead businesses to be less profitable?

"*It is essential that within a business the legitimate pursuit of profit should be in harmony with the irrenounceable protection of the dignity of the people who work at different levels in the same company.* These two goals are not in the least contrary to one another, since, on the one hand, it would not be realistic to try to guarantee the firm's future without the production of useful goods and services and without making a profit, which is the fruit of the economic activity undertaken. On the other hand, allowing workers to develop themselves fosters increased productivity and efficiency in the very work undertaken."

—Pontifical Council for Justice and Peace, *Compendium of the Social Doctrine of the Church*, 340

"The integral development of the human person through work does not impede but rather promotes the greater productivity and efficiency of work itself, even though it may weaken consolidated power structures. A business cannot be considered only as a 'society of capital goods'; it is also a 'society of persons' in which people participate in different ways and with specific responsibilities, whether they supply the necessary capital for the company's activities or take part in such activities through their labor."

—St. John Paul II, *Centesimus annus*, 43

"When Christian morals are completely observed, they yield of themselves a certain measure of prosperity to material existence."

—Leo XIII, *Rerum novarum*, 42

18. What is the foundational principle of Catholic social doctrine?

"We are convinced that 'man is the source, the focus and the aim of all economic and social life.'"

—Francis, *Laudato Si*, 127 (quoting Second Vatican Council, *Gaudium et Spes*, 63)

"The Church's social doctrine ... is based on man's creation 'in the image of God' (Gn 1:27), a datum which gives rise to the inviolable dignity of the human person and the transcendent value of natural moral norms."

—Benedict XVI, *Caritas in veritate*, 45

"This [social] teaching rests on one basic principle: individual human beings are the foundation, the cause and the end [purpose] of every social institution. That is necessarily so, for men are by nature social beings. This fact must be recognized, as also the fact that they are raised in the plan of Providence to an order of reality which is above nature."

—St. John XXIII, *Mater et magistra*, 219

19. Do the principles of Catholic social teaching apply only to Catholics?

"The Church's social teaching argues on the basis of reason and natural law, namely, on the basis of what is in accord with the nature of every human being."

—Benedict XVI, *Deus caritas est*, 28

"The principles [of Catholic social doctrine] she gives are of universal application, for they take human nature into account, and the varying conditions in which man's life is lived. They also take into account the principal characteristics of contemporary society, and are thus acceptable to all."

—St. John XXIII, *Mater et magistra*, 220

20. How do we implement these principles when working with non-Catholics?

"In today's complex situation, not least because of the growth of a globalized economy, the Church's social doctrine has become a set of fundamental guidelines offering approaches that are valid even beyond the confines of the Church: in the face of ongoing development these guidelines need to be addressed in the context of dialogue with all those seriously concerned for humanity and for the world in which we live."

—Benedict XVI, *Deus caritas est*, 27

"For Christian witness to be effective, especially in these delicate and controversial areas, it is important that special efforts be made to explain properly the reasons for the Church's position, stressing that it is not a case of imposing on non-believers a vision based on faith, but of interpreting and defending the values rooted in the very nature of the human person. In this way charity will necessarily become service to culture, politics, the economy and the family, so that the fundamental principles upon which depend the destiny of human beings and the future of civilization will be everywhere respected."

—St. John Paul II, *Novo millennio ineunte*, 51

"In their economic and social activities, Catholics often come into contact with others who do not share their view of life. In such circumstances, they must, of course, bear themselves as Catholics and do nothing to compromise religion and morality. Yet at the same time they should show themselves animated by a spirit of understanding and unselfishness, ready to cooperate loyally in achieving objects which are good in themselves, or can be turned to good."

—St. John XXIII, *Mater et magistra*, 239

21. Does Catholic social teaching apply only at the level of principle, with the practical application always left to the laity?

"The Church's teachings concerning contingent situations are subject to new and further developments and can be open to discussion, yet we cannot help but be concrete—without presuming to enter into details—lest the great social principles remain mere generalities which challenge no one. There is a need to draw practical conclusions, so that they 'will have greater impact on the complexities of current situations.'"

—Francis, *Evangelii Gaudium*, 182 (quoting Pontifical Council for Justice and
Peace, *Compendium of the Social Doctrine of the Church*, 9)

"The Church has the right and obligation not merely to guard ethical and religious principles, but also to declare its authoritative judgment in the matter of putting these principles into practice."

—St. John XXIII, *Mater et magistra*, 239

22. How are we to apply the principles of Catholic social teaching to particular business practices?

"There are three stages which should normally be followed in the reduction of social principles into practice. First, one reviews the concrete situation; secondly, one forms a judgment on it in the light of these same principles; thirdly, one decides what in the circumstances can and should be done to implement these principles. These are the three stages that are usually expressed in the three terms: look, judge, act."

—St. John XXIII, *Mater et magistra*, 236

23. Who bears responsibility for fulfilling the principles of Catholic social teaching?

"The direct duty to work for a just ordering of society...is proper to the lay faithful. As citizens of the State, they are called to take part in public life in a personal capacity. So they cannot relinquish their participation 'in the many different economic, social, legislative, administrative and cultural areas, which are intended to promote organically and institutionally the *common good*.'"

—Benedict XVI, *Deus caritas est*, 29 (quoting St. John Paul II,
Christifideles laici, 42)

"The first act of the Christian business leader, as of all Christians, is to receive; more specifically, to receive what God has done for him or her. This act of receptivity, particularly for business leaders, can be particularly difficult. As a group, business leaders tend to be more active than receptive, especially now in a globalized economy, under the effects of sophisticated communications technologies and the financialization of business. Yet without receptivity in their lives, business leaders can be tempted by a quasi-Nietzschean 'superman' complex. The temptation for some is to regard themselves as determining and creating their own principles, not as receiving them. Business leaders may only see themselves as creative, innovative, active, and constructive, but if they neglect the dimension of receiving, they distort their place within the world and overestimate their own achievements and work."

—Pontifical Council for Justice and Peace, *Vocation of the Business Leader,* 66

"It is not the role of the Pastors of the Church to intervene directly in the political structuring and organization of social life. This task is part of the vocation of the lay faithful, acting on their own initiative with their fellow citizens. Social action can assume various concrete forms. It should always have the common good in view and be in conformity with the message of the Gospel and the teaching of the Church. It is the role of the laity 'to animate temporal realities with Christian commitment, by which they show that they are witnesses and agents of peace and justice.'"

—*Catechism of the Catholic Church,* 2442 (586) (quoting St. John Paul II, *Sollicitudo rei socialis,* 47)

24. What are the responsibilities of lay Catholics for fulfilling the principles of Catholic social teaching?

"The mission of the lay faithful is therefore to configure social life correctly, respecting its legitimate autonomy and cooperating with other citizens according to their respective competences and fulfilling their own responsibility.... Charity must animate the entire lives of the lay faithful and therefore also their political activity, lived as 'social charity.'"

—Benedict XVI, *Deus caritas est*, 29

"Charitable acts must not replace the commitment to social justice.... Justice and charity are the two inseparable aspects of the single social commitment of Christians. It is incumbent on lay faithful in particular to work for a just order in society, taking part in public life in the first person, cooperating with other citizens and fulfilling their own responsibility."

—Benedict XVI, address to Italian Christian executives (March 4, 2006)

"Christians charged with responsibility in the business world are challenged to combine the legitimate pursuit of profit with a deeper concern for the spread of solidarity."

—St. John Paul II, message to participants in the conference "The Business Executive: Social Responsibility and Globalization" (March 3, 2004)

"Since they have an active role to play in the whole life of the Church, laymen are not only bound to penetrate the world with a Christian spirit, but are also called to be witnesses to Christ in all things in the midst of human society."

—*Gaudium et spes*, 43

"Christians who take an active part in present-day socio-economic development and fight for justice and charity should be convinced that they can make a great contribution to the prosperity of mankind and to the peace of the world."

—*Gaudium et spes*, 72

"The laity must take up the renewal of the temporal order as their own special obligation. Led by the light of the Gospel and the mind of the Church and motivated by Christian charity, they must act directly and in a definite way in the temporal sphere. As citizens they must cooperate with other citizens with their own particular skill and on their own responsibility. Everywhere and in all things they must seek the justice of God's kingdom."

—*Apostolicam actuositatem*, 7

"The apostolate in the social milieu, that is, the effort to infuse a Christian spirit into the mentality, customs, laws, and structures of the community in which one lives, is so much the duty and responsibility of the laity that it can never be performed properly by others. In this area the laity can exercise the apostolate of like toward like. It is here that they complement the testimony of life with the testimony of the Word. It is here where they work or practice their profession or study or reside or spend their leisure time or have their companionship that they are more capable of helping their brethren."

—*Apostolicam actuositatem*, 13

25. What should lay people aspire to in fulfilling
these principles?

"The temporal order must be renewed in such a way that, without detriment to its own proper laws, it may be brought into conformity with the higher principles of the Christian life and adapted to the shifting circumstances of time, place, and peoples."

—*Apostolicam actuositatem*, 7

26. What specific responsibilities do lay people have
within the economy?

"The initiative of lay Christians is necessary especially when the matter involves discovering or inventing the means for permeating social, political, and economic realities with the demands of Christian doctrine and life. This initiative is a normal element of the life of the Church."

—*Catechism of the Catholic Church*, 899 (238)

"In the context of the transformations taking place in the world of economy and work which are a cause of concern, the lay faithful have the responsibility of being in the forefront in working out a solution to the very serious problems of growing unemployment; to fight for the most opportune overcoming of numerous injustices that come from organizations of work which lack a proper goal; to make the workplace become a community of persons respected in their uniqueness and in their right to participation; to develop new solidarity among those that participate in a common work; to raise up new forms of entrepreneurship and to look again at systems of commerce, finance and exchange of technology."

—St. John Paul II, *Christifideles laici*, 43

Moral Dilemmas in Business

27. Is it ever acceptable to do something immoral in business in order to achieve a greater good (e.g., prevent the company from going bankrupt and save thousands of jobs)?

"One may never do evil so that good may result from it."

—*Catechism of the Catholic Church*, 1789 (441)

"Hence human activity cannot be judged as morally good merely because it is a means for attaining one or another of its goals, or simply because the subject's intention is good.... If the object of the concrete action is not in harmony with the true good of the person, the choice of that action makes our will and ourselves morally evil, thus putting us in conflict with our ultimate end, the supreme good, God himself."

—St. John Paul II, *Veritatis splendor*, 72.

"Profit is a regulator of the life of a business, but it is not the only one; *other human and moral factors* must also be considered which, in the long run, are at least equally important for the life of a business."

—St. John Paul II, *Centesimus annus*, 35

28. What if we are forced (by law, or by company policy) to do something that is intrinsically evil (e.g., dispense contraceptive products)?

"The passing of unjust laws often raises difficult problems of conscience for morally upright people with regard to the issue of cooperation, since they have a right to demand not to be forced to take part in morally evil actions. Sometimes the choices which have to be made are difficult; they may require the sacrifice of prestigious professional positions or the relinquishing of reasonable hopes of career advancement.... To refuse to take part in committing an injustice is not only a moral duty; it is also a basic human right."

—St. John Paul II, *Evangelium vitae*, 74

29. Does that mean that we can have absolutely no involvement with anything that has any evil aspect in business?

Editors' note: The Church draws a distinction between formal and material cooperation with evil. Formal cooperation occurs when the intention or action itself is intrinsically evil, and is always forbidden. Material cooperation is where the intention and action are not intrinsically evil. Material cooperation should be avoided if possible but is permissible to avoid a greater evil.

"It is necessary to recall the general principles concerning cooperation in evil actions. Christians, like all people of good will, are called upon under grave obligation of conscience not to cooperate formally in practices which, even if permitted by civil legislation, are contrary to God's law. Indeed, from the moral standpoint, it is never licit to cooperate formally in evil. Such cooperation occurs when an action, either by its very nature or by the form it takes in a concrete situation, can be defined as a direct participation in an act against innocent human life or a sharing in the immoral intention of the person committing it. This cooperation can never be justified either by invoking respect for the freedom of others or by appealing to the fact that civil law permits it or requires it. Each individual in fact has moral responsibility for the acts which he personally performs; no one can be exempted from this responsibility, and on the basis of it everyone will be judged by God himself (cf. Rom 2:6; 14:12)."

—St. John Paul II, *Evangelium vitae*, 74

"The first fundamental distinction to be made is that between formal and material cooperation. Formal cooperation is carried out when the moral agent cooperates with the immoral action of another person, sharing in the latter's evil intention. On the other hand, when a moral agent cooperates with the immoral action of another person, without sharing his/her evil intention, it is a case of material cooperation....

"Formal cooperation is always morally illicit because it represents a form of direct and intentional participation in the sinful action of another person. Material cooperation can sometimes be illicit (depending on the conditions of the 'double effect' or 'indirect voluntary' action), but when immediate material cooperation concerns grave attacks on human life, it is always to be considered illicit, given the precious nature of the value in question."

—Pontifical Academy for Life, "Moral Reflections on Vaccines Prepared from Cells Derived from Aborted Human Foetuses" (June 5, 2005)

— 2 —

Finance and Investing

Profit

30. Is it morally acceptable to make a profit?

"Naturally, profit is legitimate and, in just measure, necessary for economic development."

—Benedict XVI, Angelus (September 23, 2007)

"The Church acknowledges the legitimate *role of profit* as an indication that a business is functioning well."

—St. John Paul II, *Centesimus annus*, 35

"Profits are necessary.... They make possible the investments that ensure the future of a business and they guarantee employment."

—*Catechism of the Catholic Church*, 2432 (584)

31. Is the main purpose of a business to make profit?

"Business is a vocation, and a noble vocation, provided that those engaged in it see themselves challenged by a greater meaning in life; this will enable them truly to serve the common good by striving to increase the goods of this world and to make them more accessible to all."

—Francis, *Evangelii Gaudium*, 203

"Business is a noble vocation, directed to producing wealth and improving our world. It can be a fruitful source of prosperity for the areas in which it operates, especially if it sees the creation of jobs as an essential part of its service to the common good."

—Francis, *Laudato Si*, 129

"The purpose of a business firm is not simply to make a profit, but is to be found in its very existence as a *community of persons* who in various ways are endeavoring to satisfy their basic needs, and who form a particular group at the service of the whole of society."

—St. John Paul II, *Centesimus annus*, 35

32. Is it morally acceptable to seek to maximize profit—in the sense of pursuing profit ahead of everything else?

"The principle of the maximization of profits, frequently isolated from other considerations, reflects a misunderstanding of the very concept of the economy."

—Francis, *Laudato Si*, 195

"It should always be kept in mind that 'environmental protection cannot be assured solely on the basis of financial calculations of costs and benefits. The environment is one of those goods that cannot be adequately safeguarded or promoted by market forces.' Once more, we need to reject a magical conception of the market, which would suggest that problems can be solved simply by an increase in the profits of companies or individuals. Is it realistic to hope that those who are obsessed with maximizing profits will stop to reflect on the environmental damage which they will leave behind for future generations?"

—Francis, *Laudato Si*, 190 (quoting Pontifical Council for Justice and Peace, *Compendium of the Social Doctrine of the Church*, 470.)

"Growth in justice requires more than economic growth, while presupposing such growth: it requires decisions, programs, mechanisms and processes specifically geared to a better distribution of income, the creation of sources of employment and an integral promotion of the poor which goes beyond a simple welfare mentality. I am far from proposing an irresponsible populism, but the economy can no longer turn to remedies that are a new poison, such as attempting to increase profits by reducing the work force and thereby adding to the ranks of the excluded."

—Francis, *Evangelii Gaudium*, 204

"Concern with the idols of power, profit, and money, rather than with the value of the human person, has become a basic norm for functioning and a crucial criterion for organization. We have forgotten and are still forgetting that over and above business, logic and the parameters of the market is the human being; and that something is [due to] men and women in as much as they are human beings by virtue of their profound dignity: to offer them the possibility of living a dignified life and of actively participating in the common good."

—Francis, address to the Centesimus Annus Pro Pontifice Foundation (May 25, 2013)

"A theory that makes profit the exclusive norm and ultimate end of economic activity is morally unacceptable."

—*Catechism of the Catholic Church*, 2424 (582)

"Starvation and ecological emergencies stand to denounce, with increasing evidence, that the logic of profit, if it prevails, increases the disproportion between rich and poor and leads to a ruinous exploitation of the planet."

—Benedict XVI, Angelus (September 23, 2007)

"Christians charged with responsibility in the business world are challenged to combine the legitimate pursuit of profit with a deeper concern for the spread of solidarity."

—St. John Paul II, message to participants in the conference "The Business Executive: Social Responsibility and Globalization" (March 3, 2004)

"In the domain of social economy the duty pressing for attention is the judicious adjustment of production to consumption on the basis of human needs and human dignity. In view of this urgency, the question which comes to the fore today is that of the organization and equipment of the social economy at its production-stage. The solution of this question must not be sought from the theory of 'laws of the market'—a purely positivistic by-product of neo-Kantian criticism—nor in the mere formula, every bit as artificial, of 'full employment.' There before you is the problem on which We should like to see the theorists and practical men of the Catholic social movement concentrate their attention and bring their studies to bear."

—Pius XII, "Production for Human Needs," address prepared for delegates to the Catholic International Congresses for Social Study and Social Action (June 3, 1950)[1]

1. *The Catholic Mind*, August 1950, 507–10.

33. Do we have a moral obligation to protect
    the capital that is entrusted to us as investment
    in our business?

"Man, to whom, in Genesis, God entrusted the earth, has the
duty to make all the earth's goods fruitful, committing himself
to use them to satisfy the multiple needs of each member of
the human family. One of the recurring metaphors of the Gospel is, in effect, exactly that of the steward. With the heart of
a faithful administrator man must, therefore, administer the
resources entrusted to him by God, putting them at the dispo-
sition of all."

> —Benedict XVI, address to members of the Centesimus Annus—Pro
> Pontifice Foundation (May 31, 2008)

"The laws passed to promote corporate business, while dividing
and limiting the risk of business, have given occasion to the
most sordid license.... Directors of business companies, for-
getful of their trust, betray the rights of those whose savings
they have undertaken to administer."

> —Pius XI, *Quadragesimo anno*, 132

34. What should we do if we face a choice between
    immoral activity and allowing a significant loss to the
    capital that was entrusted to us?

See the section "Moral Dilemmas in Business" in chapter 1.

35. How much of our own personal profits should we be
    willing to sacrifice in order to avoid or reduce layoffs
    during an economic downturn?

"In economic matters, respect for human dignity requires the
practice of the virtue of *temperance,* to moderate our attach-

ment to the goods of this world; of the virtue of *justice,* to preserve our neighbor's rights and to render what is his or her due; and of *solidarity,* following the golden rule and in keeping with the generosity of the Lord, who 'though he was rich, yet for your sake...became poor, so that by his poverty you might become rich' (2 Cor 8:9)."

—*Catechism of the Catholic Church,* 2407 (578)

"No one, certainly, is obliged to assist others out of what is required for his own necessary use or for that of his family, or even to give to others what he himself needs to maintain his station in life becomingly and decently....But when the demands of necessity and propriety have been sufficiently met, it is a duty to give to the poor out of that which remains."

—Leo XIII, *Rerum novarum,* 36

Investment

36. In deciding what capital investments to make, such as where to build a new manufacturing plant, should we take into account any other considerations beyond what is going to reap the most profit for the firm?

"Goods of production—material or immaterial—such as land, factories, practical or artistic skills, oblige their possessors to employ them in ways that will benefit the greatest number."

—*Catechism of the Catholic Church,* 2405 (578)

"Those *responsible for business enterprises* are responsible to society for the economic and ecological effects of their operations. [footnote reference to *Centesimus Annus,* 48] They have an obligation to consider the good of persons and not only the increase of *profits*."

—*Catechism of the Catholic Church*, 2432 (584)

"Even the decision to invest in one place rather than another, in one productive sector rather than another, is always a moral and cultural choice. Given the utter necessity of certain economic conditions and of political stability, the decision to invest, that is, to offer people an opportunity to make good use of their own labor, is also determined by an attitude of human sympathy and trust in Providence, which reveal the human quality of the person making such decisions."

—St. John Paul II, *Centesimus annus*, 36

"Development cannot consist only in the use, dominion over and indiscriminate possession of created things and the products of human industry, but rather in subordinating the possession, dominion and use to man's divine likeness and to his vocation to immortality."

—St. John Paul II, *Sollicitudo rei socialis*, 29

"True development must be based on the love of God and neighbor, and must help to promote the relationships between individuals and society."

—St. John Paul II, *Sollicitudo rei socialis*, 33

"Investments, for their part, must be directed toward procuring employment and sufficient income for the people both now and in the future. Whoever makes decisions concerning these investments and the planning of the economy—whether they be individuals or groups of public authorities—are bound to keep these objectives in mind and to recognize their serious obligation of watching, on the one hand, that provision be made for the necessities required for a decent life both of individuals and of the whole community and, on the other, of looking out for the future and of establishing a right balance between the needs of present-day consumption, both individual and collective, and the demands of investing for the generation to come. They should also always bear in mind the urgent needs of underdeveloped countries or regions. In monetary matters they should beware of hurting the welfare of their own country or of other countries. Care should also be taken lest the economically weak countries unjustly suffer any loss from a change in the value of money."

—*Gaudium et spes*, 70

"Whoever has received from the bounty of God a greater share of goods, whether corporeal and external, or of the soul, has received them for this purpose, namely, that he employ them for his own perfection and, likewise, as a servant of Divine Providence, for the benefit of others."

—Leo XIII, *Rerum novarum*, 36

37. Are there any moral considerations when deciding whether to focus on shorter- or longer-term issues in finance?

"Objectively, the most important function of finance is to sustain the possibility of long-term investment and hence of development.... The recent crisis demonstrates how financial activity can at times be completely turned in on itself, lacking any long-term consideration of the common good. This lowering of the objectives of global finance to the very short term reduces its capacity to function as a bridge between the present and the future, and as a stimulus to the creation of new opportunities for production and for work in the long term. Finance limited in this way to the short and very short term becomes dangerous for everyone, even for those who benefit when the markets perform well."

—Benedict XVI, message for World Day of Peace 2009, 10

Taxes

38. Is it morally acceptable to minimize the amount of taxes our firm must pay through offshore tax havens or other loopholes in the tax code?

"I encourage financial experts and political leaders to ponder the words of one of the sages of antiquity: 'Not to share one's wealth with the poor is to steal from them and to take away their livelihood. It is not our own goods which we hold, but theirs.'"

—Francis, *Evangelii Gaudium*, 57 (quoting Saint John Chrysostom, *De Lazaro Concio*, II, 6: PG 48, 992D)

"It grows increasingly true that the obligations of justice and love are fulfilled only if each person, contributing to the common good, according to his own abilities and the needs of others, also promotes and assists the public and private institutions dedicated to bettering the conditions of human life. Yet there are those who, while possessing grand and rather noble sentiments, nevertheless in reality live always as if they cared nothing for the needs of society. Many in various places even make light of social laws and precepts, and do not hesitate to resort to various frauds and deceptions in avoiding just taxes or other debts due to society."

—*Gaudium et spes*, 30

"Even if it does not contradict the provisions of civil law, any form of unjustly taking and keeping the property of others is against the seventh commandment: thus, deliberate retention of goods lent or of objects lost; business fraud; paying unjust wages; forcing up prices by taking advantage of the ignorance or hardship of another. [footnote reference to Dt 25:13–16, 24:14–15; Jas 5:4; Am 8:4–6]

"The following are also morally illicit: speculation in which one contrives to manipulate the price of goods artificially in order to gain an advantage to the detriment of others; corruption in which one influences the judgment of those who must make decisions according to law;...tax evasion."

—*Catechism of the Catholic Church*, 2409 (579)

— 3 —

Management

Compensation

39. What is a "just wage"?

"In determining fair pay both the needs and the contributions of each person must be taken into account. 'Remuneration for work should guarantee man the opportunity to provide a dignified livelihood for himself and his family on the material, social, cultural and spiritual level, taking into account the role and the productivity of each, the state of the business, and the common good.'" [footnote reference to *Gaudium et spes,* 67, no. 2]

   —*Catechism of the Catholic Church,* 2434 (584–85)

"We are not simply talking about ensuring nourishment or a 'dignified sustenance' for all people, but also their 'general temporal welfare and prosperity.' This means education, access to health care, and above all employment, for it is through free, creative, participatory and mutually supportive labor that human beings express and enhance the dignity of their lives. A just wage enables them to have adequate access to all the other goods which are destined for our common use."

—Francis, *Evangelii Gaudium*, 192 (quoting John XIII, *Mater et Magistra*, 3

"A workman's wages should be sufficient to enable him to support himself, his wife and his children."

—St. John Paul II, *Centesimus annus*, 8

"Even prior to the logic of a fair exchange of goods and forms of justice appropriate to it, there exists *something which is due to man because he is a man,* by reason of his lofty dignity."

—St. John Paul II, *Centesimus annus*, 34

"Therefore, with all our strength and effort we must strive that at least in the future the abundant fruits of production will accrue equitably to those who are rich and will be distributed in ample sufficiency among the workers—not that these may become remiss in work, for man is born to labor as the bird to fly—but that they may increase their property by thrift, that they may bear, by wise management of this increase in property, the burdens of family life with greater ease and security, and that, emerging from the insecure lot in life in whose uncertainties non-owning workers are cast, they may be able not only to endure the vicissitudes of earthly existence but have also assurance that when their lives are ended they will provide in some measure for those they leave after them."

—Pius XI, *Quadragesimo Anno*, 61

40. An employee is not forced to take any particular job, so if he agrees to work for a specific wage, doesn't that agreement make the wage just?

"Agreement between the parties is not sufficient to justify morally the amount to be received in wages."

—*Catechism of the Catholic Church*, 2434 (585)

"Unfortunately, even today one finds instances of contracts between employers and employees which lack reference to the most elementary justice regarding the employment of children or women, working hours, the hygienic condition of the workplace and fair pay."

—St. John Paul II, *Centesimus annus*, 8

"Let the working man and the employer make free agreements, and in particular let them agree freely as to the wages; nevertheless, there underlies a dictate of natural justice more imperious and ancient than any bargain between man and man, namely, that wages ought not to be insufficient to support a frugal and well-behaved wage-earner. If through necessity or fear of a worse evil the workman accept harder conditions because an employer or contractor will afford him no better, he is made the victim of force and injustice."

—Leo XIII, *Rerum novarum*, 45

41. What factors should an employer consider to calculate just compensation for an employee?

"In determining fair pay both the needs and the contributions of each person must be taken into account."

—*Catechism of the Catholic Church*, 2434 (584)

"Just remuneration for the work of an adult who is responsible for a family means remuneration which will suffice for establishing and properly maintaining a family and for providing security for its future."

—St. John Paul II, *Laborem exercens*, 19

"Remuneration for labor is to be such that man may be furnished the means to cultivate worthily his own material, social, cultural, and spiritual life and that of his dependents, in view of the function and productiveness of each one, the conditions of the factory or workshop, and the common good."

—*Gaudium et spes,* 67 (a different translation from the version of this passage quoted in the *Catechism,* cited in question 1)

"In determining wages, therefore, justice demands that account be taken not only of the needs of the individual workers and their families, but also of the financial state of the business concern for which they work."

—St. John XXIII, *Mater et magistra,* 33

"[Remuneration] must be determined in accordance with justice and equity; which means that workers must be paid a wage which allows them to live a truly human life and to fulfill their family obligations in a worthy manner. Other factors too enter into the assessment of a just wage: namely, the effective contribution which each individual makes to the economic effort, the financial state of the company for which he works, the requirements of the general good of the particular country— having regard especially to the repercussions on the overall employment of the working force in the country as a whole— and finally the requirements of the common good of the universal family of nations of every kind, both large and small."

—St. John XXIII, *Mater et magistra,* 71

"But a further point needs emphasizing: Any adjustment between wages and profits must take into account the demands of the common good of the particular country and of the whole human family.

"What are these demands? On the national level they include: employment of the greatest possible number of workers; care lest privileged classes arise, even among the workers;

maintenance of equilibrium between wages and prices; the need to make goods and services accessible to the greatest number; elimination, or at least the restriction, of inequalities in the various branches of the economy—that is, between agriculture, industry and services; creation of a proper balance between economic expansion and the development of social services, especially through the activity of public authorities; the best possible adjustment of the means of production to the progress of science and technology; seeing to it that the benefits which make possible a more human way of life will be available not merely to the present generation but to the coming generations as well."

—St. John XXIII, *Mater et magistra*, 78–79

"The worker must be paid a wage sufficient to support him and his family."

—Pius XI, *Quadragesimo anno*, 71

"In determining the amount of the wage, the condition of a business and of the one carrying it on must also be taken into account; for it would be unjust to demand excessive wages which a business cannot stand without its ruin and consequent calamity to the workers."

—Pius XI, *Quadragesimo anno*, 72

"The amount of the pay must be adjusted to the public economic good...namely, that the opportunity to work be provided to those who are able and willing to work. This opportunity depends largely on the wage and salary rate, which can help as long as it is kept within proper limits, but which on the other hand can be an obstacle if it exceeds these limits. For everyone knows that an excessive lowering of wages, or their increase beyond due measure, causes unemployment.... Hence it is contrary to social justice when, for the sake of personal gain and without regard for the common good, wages and salaries are excessively lowered or raised; and this same social justice demands that wages and salaries be so managed, through agreement of plans and wills, in so far as can be done, as to offer to the greatest possible number the opportunity of getting work and obtaining suitable means of livelihood."

—Pius XI, *Quadragesimo anno*, 74

"It is a most sacred law of nature that a father should provide food and all necessaries for those whom he has begotten; and, similarly, it is natural that he should wish that his children, who carry on, so to speak, and continue his personality, should be by him provided with all that is needful to enable them to keep themselves decently from want and misery amid the uncertainties of this mortal life."

—Leo XIII, *Rerum novarum*, 13

42. Whose responsibility is it to see that a just wage is paid?

"[Just] remuneration can be given either through what is called a *family wage*—that is, a single salary given to the head of the family for his work, sufficient for the needs of the family without the other spouse having to take up gainful employment outside the home—or through *other social measures* such as family allowances or grants to mothers devoting themselves exclusively to their families. These grants should correspond to the actual needs, that is, to the number of dependents for as long as they are not in a position to assume proper responsibility for their own lives."

—St. John Paul II, *Laborem exercens*, 19

"The State...has the task of determining the juridical framework within which economic affairs are to be conducted, and thus of safeguarding the prerequisites of a free economy, which presumes a certain equality between the parties, such that one party would not be so powerful as practically to reduce the other to subservience."

—St. John Paul II, *Centesimus annus*, 15

"The State must contribute to the achievement of...[unemployment support, adequate wage levels, humane working conditions] both directly and indirectly. Indirectly and according to the *principle of subsidiarity*, by creating favorable conditions for the free exercise of economic activity.... Directly and according to the *principle of solidarity*, by defending the weakest, by placing certain limits on the autonomy of the parties who determine working conditions, and by ensuring in every case the necessary minimum support for the unemployed worker."

—St. John Paul II, *Centesimus annus*, 15

"It is the duty of society, moreover, according to the circumstances prevailing in it, and in keeping with its role, to help the citizens to find sufficient employment."

—*Gaudium et spes*, 67

"We therefore consider it Our duty to reaffirm that the remuneration of work is not something that can be left to the laws of the marketplace; nor should it be a decision left to the will of the more powerful. It must be determined in accordance with justice and equity; which means that workers must be paid a wage which allows them to live a truly human life and to fulfill their family obligations in a worthy manner."

—St. John XXIII, *Mater et magistra*, 71

"To defraud any one of wages that are his due is a great crime which cries to the avenging anger of Heaven."

—Leo XIII, *Rerum novarum*, 20

"Let the working man and the employer make free agreements, and in particular let them agree freely as to the wages; nevertheless, there underlies a dictate of natural justice more imperious and ancient than any bargain between man and man, namely, that wages ought not to be insufficient to support a frugal and well-behaved wage-earner."

—Leo XIII, *Rerum novarum*, 45

43. Is it moral to pay employees more than they could get elsewhere for the same work, for the sake of paying a living wage, if in doing so we would reduce the amount of profits that the firm would earn otherwise?

"Just remuneration for the work of an adult who is responsible for a family means remuneration which will suffice for establishing and properly maintaining a family and for providing security for its future."

—St. John Paul II, *Laborem exercens*, 19

"In determining the amount of the wage, the condition of a business and of the one carrying it on must also be taken into account; for it would be unjust to demand excessive wages which a business cannot stand without its ruin and consequent calamity to the workers."

—Pius XI, *Quadragesimo anno*, 72

44. Should employers provide their firm's employees
with a share in the ownership of the company?

"[Catholic social teaching] recognizes the legitimacy of workers' efforts to obtain full respect for their dignity and to gain
broader areas of participation in the life of industrial enterprises so that, while cooperating with others and under the
direction of others, they can in a certain sense 'work for themselves' through the exercise of their intelligence and freedom."

—St. John Paul II, *Centesimus annus,* 43

"We must notice in this connection the system of self-financ-
ing adopted in many countries by large, or comparatively large
firms. Because these companies are financing replacement and
plant expansion out of their own profits, they grow at a very
rapid rate. In such cases We believe that the workers should
be allocated shares in the firms for which they work, especially
when they are paid no more than a minimum wage."

—St. John XXIII, *Mater et magistra,* 75

"It is especially desirable today that workers gradually come to
share in the ownership of their company, by ways and in the
manner that seem most suitable."

—St. John XXIII, *Mater et magistra,* 77

"She regards with approval and favors everything which, within
the limits permitted by circumstances, aims at introducing the
elements of a partnership contract *(contrato de sociedad)* into
the wage contract *(contrato de trabajo),* and betters the general condition of the worker. The Church likewise counsels all
to use whatever contributes toward making relations between
employer and workers more human, more Christian and more
conducive to mutual confidence. The class struggle can never

be a social end. The discussions between employers and workers must have as their main aim peace and collaboration.

—Pius XII, "The Church's Concern for Economic Life," radio address to the
Catholic men of Spain, employers and workers (March 11, 1951)

"The immense multitude of the non-owning workers on the one hand and the enormous riches of certain very wealthy men on the other establish an unanswerable argument that the riches which are so abundantly produced in our age of 'industrialism,' as it is called, are not rightly distributed and equitably made available to the various classes of the people.

"Therefore, with all our strength and effort we must strive that at least in the future the abundant fruits of production will accrue equitably to those who are rich and will be distributed in ample sufficiency among the workers—not that these may become remiss in work, for man is born to labor as the bird to fly—but that they may increase their property by thrift, that they may bear, by wise management of this increase in property, the burdens of family life with greater ease and security, and that, emerging from the insecure lot in life in whose uncertainties non-owning workers are cast, they may be able not only to endure the vicissitudes of earthly existence but have also assurance that when their lives are ended they will provide in some measure for those they leave after them."

—Pius XI, *Quadragesimo anno*, 60–61

45. What compensation levels are appropriate for senior executives?

"It is precisely the ability to foresee both the needs of others and the combinations of productive factors most adapted to satisfying those needs that constitutes another important source of wealth in modern society. Besides, many goods cannot be adequately produced through the work of an isolated individual; they require the cooperation of many people in working towards a common goal. Organizing such a productive effort, planning its duration in time, making sure that it corresponds in a positive way to the demands which it must satisfy, and taking the necessary risks—all this too is a source of wealth in today's society. In this way, the *role* of disciplined and creative *human work* and, as an essential part of that work, *initiative and entrepreneurial ability*, becomes increasingly evident and decisive."

—St. John Paul II, *Centesimus annus*, 32

"These demands of the common good,[1] both on a national and a world level, must also be borne in mind when assessing the rate of return due as compensation to the company's management, and as interest or dividends to investors."

—St. John XXIII, *Mater et magistra*, 81

"But not every distribution among human beings of property and wealth is of a character to attain either completely or to a satisfactory degree of perfection the end which God intends.

---

1. "What are these demands? On the national level they include: employment of the greatest possible number of workers; care lest privileged classes arise, even among the workers; maintenance of equilibrium between wages and prices; the need to make goods and services accessible to the greatest number; elimination, or at least the restriction, of inequalities in the various branches of the economy—that is, between agriculture, industry and services; creation of a proper balance between economic expansion and the development of social services, especially through the activity of public authorities; the best possible adjustment of the means of production to the progress of science and technology; seeing to it that the benefits which make possible a more human way of life will be available not merely to the present generation but to the coming generations as well." St. John XXIII, *Mater et magistra*, 79.

Therefore, the riches that economic-social developments constantly increase ought to be so distributed among individual persons and classes that the common advantage of all, which Leo XIII had praised, will be safeguarded; in other words, that the common good of all society will be kept inviolate. By this law of social justice, one class is forbidden to exclude the other from sharing in the benefits. Hence the class of the wealthy violates this law no less, when, as if free from care on account of its wealth, it thinks it the right order of things for it to get everything and the worker nothing, than does the non-owning working class when, angered deeply at outraged justice and too ready to assert wrongly the one right it is conscious of, it demands for itself everything as if produced by its own hands....

"To each, therefore, must be given his own share of goods, and the distribution of created goods, which, as every discerning person knows, is laboring today under the gravest evils due to the huge disparity between the few exceedingly rich and the unnumbered propertyless, must be effectively called back to and brought into conformity with the norms of the common good, that is, social justice."

—Pius XI, *Quadragesimo anno*, 57–58

"Those who are engaged in producing goods, therefore, are not forbidden to increase their fortune in a just and lawful manner; for it is only fair that he who renders service to the community and makes it richer should also, through the increased wealth of the community, be made richer himself according to his position, provided that all these things be sought with due respect for the laws of God and without impairing the rights of others and that they be employed in accordance with faith and right reason."

—Pius XI, *Quadragesimo anno*, 136

46. Should we take an employee's personal circumstances into consideration when deciding his compensation (e.g., should a married man with a large family receive greater compensation than a single man, if both are doing exactly the same job)?

"In determining fair pay both the needs and the contributions of each person must be taken into account."

—*Catechism of the Catholic Church*, 2434 (584)

"[Remuneration] must be determined in accordance with justice and equity; which means that workers must be paid a wage which allows them to live a truly human life and to fulfill their family obligations in a worthy manner. Other factors too enter into the assessment of a just wage: namely, the effective contribution which each individual makes to the economic effort."

—St. John XXIII, *Mater et magistra*, 71

"It is an intolerable abuse, and to be abolished at all cost, for mothers on account of the father's low wage to be forced to engage in gainful occupations outside the home to the neglect of their proper cares and duties, especially the training of children."

—Pius XI, *Quadragesimo anno*, 71

Benefits

47. Is there a specific level of healthcare benefits that we are morally obliged to offer our employees?

"The expenses involved in health care, especially in the case of accidents at work, demand that medical assistance should be easily available for workers, and that as far as possible it should be cheap or even free of charge."

—St. John Paul II, *Laborem exercens*, 19

48. Is it morally acceptable to offer employees healthcare benefits that cover abortion or birth control?

"Christians, like all people of good will, are called upon under grave obligation of conscience not to cooperate formally in practices which, even if permitted by civil legislation, are contrary to God's law.... Such cooperation occurs when an action, either by its very nature or by the form it takes in a concrete situation, can be defined as a direct participation in an act against innocent human life or a sharing in the immoral intention of the person committing it."

—St. John Paul II, *Evangelium vitae*, 74

"Formal cooperation is always morally illicit because it represents a form of direct and intentional participation in the sinful action of another person. Material cooperation can sometimes be illicit...but when immediate material cooperation concerns grave attacks on human life, it is always to be considered illicit, given the precious nature of the value in question."

—Pontifical Academy for Life, "Moral Reflections on Vaccines Prepared from Cells Derived from Aborted Human Foetuses" (June 5, 2005)

49. Is it morally acceptable to extend spousal healthcare benefits to cohabitating companions of our employees?

"Equality before the law must respect the principle of justice which means treating equals equally, and what is different differently: i.e., to give each one his due in justice. This principle of justice would be violated if de facto unions were given a juridical treatment similar or equivalent to the family based on marriage. If the family based on marriage and de facto unions are neither similar nor equivalent in their duties, functions and services in society, then they cannot be similar or equivalent in their juridical status."

—Pontifical Council for the Family, "Family, Marriage, and 'De Facto' Unions," 10

"In the search for justified solutions in modern society, the family cannot be put on the same level as mere associations or unions, and the latter cannot enjoy the particular rights exclusively connected with the protection of the conjugal commitment and the family based on marriage, a stable community of life and love, the result of the total and faithful gift of the spouses, open to life."

—St. John Paul II, discourse to the second meeting of European politicians and lawmakers, Pontifical Council for the Family, Vatican City (October 23, 1998), quoted in "Family, Marriage, and 'De Facto' Unions," 17

50. Is it morally acceptable to extend spousal healthcare benefits to homosexual partners of our employees?

"In those situations where homosexual unions have been legally recognized or have been given the legal status and rights belonging to marriage, clear and emphatic opposition is a duty. One must refrain from any kind of formal cooperation in the enactment or application of such gravely unjust laws and, as far as possible, from material cooperation on the level of their application. In this area, everyone can exercise the right to conscientious objection."

—Congregation for the Doctrine of the Faith, "Considerations Regarding Proposals to Give Legal Recognition to Unions Between Homosexual Persons," 5

Working Conditions

51. What general working conditions should be given
to employees?

"Employees are not mere 'human resources' or 'human capital.' Consequently, work must be designed for the capacities and qualities of human beings, and so we must not simply require that people adapt to their work as if they were machines. Good work gives scope for the intelligence and freedom of workers, its context promotes social relationships and real collaboration, and it does not damage the health and physical well-being of the worker."

—Pontifical Council for Justice and Peace, *Vocation of the Business Leader,* 46

"An indispensable prerequisite for the success of any small business enterprise is that the employer should be able to depend upon the faithful collaboration of his employees. Let Us say at once that the employer himself is the deciding factor in this; he is the principal source of the spirit which animates his employees. If he is noticeably careful to place the interests of all concerned above his own private interests, he will have little difficulty in maintaining the same spirit among his subordinates. The latter will readily understand that their superior, under whose orders they do their work, has no intention of profiting unjustly at their expense, or of exploiting their labor excessively. On the other hand, they will see that, by providing them and their families with the means of livelihood, he is likewise affording them an opportunity to perfect their own individual capacities, to engage in work that is useful and profitable, and to contribute according to their abilities to the service of the community as well as to their own economic and moral improvement."

—Pius XII, address to the First National Congress of Small Industry (January 20, 1956)[2]

52. What obligations do we have to ensure the health and safety of our employees as they do their work, beyond the legal (e.g., U.S. Occupational Safety and Health Act of 1970) requirements?

"Among these rights [of employees] there should never be overlooked the right to a working environment and to manufacturing processes which are not harmful to the workers' physical health or to their moral integrity."

—St. John Paul II, *Laborem exercens*, 19

"The conditions in which a man works...must not be such as to weaken his physical or moral fiber, or militate against the proper development of adolescents to manhood."

—St. John XXIII, *Pacem in terris*, 19

"Every human work entails a certain risk, whether physical, economic, or moral; this risk may, or even must, be accepted, when it does not pass the limits set by prudence. Indeed, man finds a powerful psychological stimulus in this sort of challenge. On the other hand, however, no one may, without serious reasons, compromise his own health or that of his fellows, risk his own life or that of others. And yet how much imprudence, how much culpable negligence, how many risks deliberately increased, occur as a result of the sole desire of avoiding the economic charges and material sacrifices presupposed by every ap-

2. *The Pope Speaks*, Spring–Summer 1956, 49–52.

plication of safety measures? The line of least resistance in this case is the same for all: in order to avoid waste of time and to increase production and profit, or even simply to save oneself an unpleasant psychological effort, all vigilance is relaxed and sometimes even the most elementary precautions are neglected.

"If, however, we consider recent social evolution and reflect a little, it is easy to perceive the real good and utility of such an effort. No one nowadays denies the part played in the worker's productivity by his subjective dispositions. Non-recognition of the physical, affective, and moral requirements of the human being ends by embittering him and turning him against those who despise his personal dignity. How can the interest each man has in his work, and the professional conscience which impels him to do it perfectly, how can these subsist, when there is constantly imminent the threat of an accident which would deprive the individual and his family of the salary on which their material sustenance depends? Even on economic grounds alone, such reasons suffice in themselves to arouse in employers the will to assure their workers of satisfactory safety and hygienic conditions.

"Among the means of a general order which are utilized for this purpose, it is certain that professional selection and training, together with the perfecting of workmanship, occupy a leading place. This fact is clearly manifested by the increased frequency of accidents among immigrant workers, who are set to industrial tasks for which they have not been prepared by long apprenticeship, nor even by family or regional traditions. When considered from this point of view, the question appears in its very vast extension, and reveals one of its typical characteristics: the specific problems of industrial accident prevention will only find complete solution when reinserted into a general plan which takes all aspects of the worker's life into account and satisfies all his lawful desires. The application of measures of a technical nature will thus be facilitated, and will produce assured results such as neither force nor other external means of persuasion could obtain. These rapid considerations suffice to illustrate the complexity of the tasks facing preventive organizations. How much patient research, skill, and cooperative spirit are required in order to solve the theoretical problems! And how can we describe the many obstacles which impede the application of safety devices! These difficulties are often attributable to the very parties concerned, who do not understand the purpose of what is asked of them or the tragic consequences of actions forbidden to them, or else, while not denying the necessity of the rules laid down, they gradually tire of observing them, so that their good will needs to be unceasingly stimulated."

—Pius XII, address to the delegates to the First World Congress on the Prevention of Industrial Accidents (April 3, 1955)[3]

"It is neither just nor human so to grind men down with excessive labor as to stupefy their minds and wear out their bodies. Man's powers, like his general nature, are limited, and beyond these limits he cannot go. His strength is developed and increased by use and exercise, but only on condition of due intermission and proper rest. Daily labor, therefore, should be so regulated as not to be protracted over longer hours than strength admits. How many and how long the intervals of rest should be must depend on the nature of the work, on circumstances of time and place, and on the health and strength of the workman."

—Leo XIII, *Rerum novarum*, 42

3. *Pius XII and Technology*, ed. Rev. Leo J. Haigerty, no. 8, 40–43.

53. Are we obliged to offer any kind of training and development opportunities to our staff if business success does not require it?

"Work becomes ever more fruitful and productive to the extent that people become more knowledgeable of the productive potentialities of the earth and more profoundly cognizant of the needs of those for whom their work is done."

—St. John Paul II, *Centesimus annus,* 31

54. Beyond legal requirements, does an employer have an obligation to take into consideration a woman's family life?

"The Church acknowledges the indispensable contribution which women make to society through the sensitivity, intuition and other distinctive skill sets which they, more than men, tend to possess ... Because 'the feminine genius is needed in all expressions in the life of society, the presence of women must also be guaranteed in the workplace' and in the various other settings where important decisions are made, both in the Church and in social structures."

—Francis, *Evangelii Gaudium,* 103 (quoting Pontifical Council for Justice and Peace, *Compendium of the Social Doctrine of the Church,* 295)

"There is no doubt that the equal dignity and responsibility of men and women fully justifies women's access to public functions. On the other hand the true advancement of women requires that clear recognition be given to the value of their maternal and family role, by comparison with all other public roles and all other professions. Furthermore, these roles and professions should be harmoniously combined, if we wish the evolution of society and culture to be truly and fully human."

—St. John Paul II, *Familiaris consortio,* 23

"In this context it should be emphasized that, on a more general level, the whole labor process must be organized and adapted in such a way as to respect the requirements of the person and his or her forms of life, above all life in the home, taking into account the individual's age and sex. It is a fact that in many societies women work in nearly every sector of life. But it is fitting that they should be able to fulfill their tasks *in accordance with their own nature*, without being discriminated against and without being excluded from jobs for which they are capable, but also without lack of respect for their family aspirations and for their specific role in contributing, together with men, to the good of society. The *true advancement of women* requires that labor should be structured in such a way that women do not have to pay for their advancement by abandoning what is specific to them and at the expense of the family, in which women as mothers have an irreplaceable role."

—St. John Paul II, *Laborem exercens*, 19

"In this regard, it cannot be forgotten that the interrelationship between these two activities—family and work—has, for women, characteristics different from those in the case of men. The harmonization of the organization of work and laws governing work with the demands stemming from the mission of women within the family is a challenge. The question is not only legal, economic and organizational; it is above all a question of mentality, culture, and respect. Indeed, a just valuing of the work of women within the family is required. In this way, women who freely desire will be able to devote the totality of their time to the work of the household without being stigmatized by society or penalized financially, while those who wish also to engage in other work may be able to do so with an appropriate work-schedule, and not have to choose between relinquishing their family life or enduring continual stress, with negative consequences for one's own equilibrium and the harmony of the family."

—Congregation for the Doctrine of the Faith, "Letter to the Bishops of the Catholic Church on the Collaboration of Men and Women in the Church and in the World," 13

"Women must be accorded such conditions of work as are consistent with their needs and responsibilities as wives and mothers."

—St. John XXIII, *Pacem in terris,* 19

55. Do we have any obligation to make allowance for employees' religious observances?

"Respect for the dignity of the person, which implies the defense and promotion of human rights, demands the recognition of the religious dimension of the individual. This is not simply a requirement 'concerning matters of faith,' but a requirement that finds itself inextricably bound up with the very reality of the individual. In fact, the individual's relation to God is a constitutive element of the very 'being' and 'existence' of an individual: it is in God that we 'live, move and have our being' (Acts 17:28). Even if not all believe this truth, the many who are convinced of it have the right to be respected for their faith and for their life-choice, individual and communal, that flows from that faith. This is the *right of freedom of conscience and religious freedom,* the effective acknowledgment of which is among the highest goods and the most serious duties of every people that truly wishes to assure the good of the person and society."

—St. John Paul II, *Christifideles laici,* 39

"The employer is bound to see that the worker has time for his religious duties."

—Leo XIII, *Rerum novarum*, 20

"The religious interests and the spiritual well-being of the workers [should] receive proper consideration."

—Leo XIII, *Rerum novarum*, 31

56. More specifically, do we have an obligation to allow employees Sundays off?

"On Sundays and other holy days of obligation, the faithful are to refrain from engaging in work or activities that hinder the worship owed to God, the joy proper to the Lord's Day, the performance of the works of mercy, and the appropriate relaxation of mind and body. [footnote reference to the *Codex Iuris Canonici,* canon 120] Family needs or important social service can legitimately excuse from the obligation of Sunday rest. The faithful should see to it that legitimate excuses do not lead to habits prejudicial to religion, family life, and health."

—*Catechism of the Catholic Church,* 2185 (527)

"Sanctifying Sunday and holy days requires a common effort. Every Christian should avoid making unnecessary demands on others that would hinder them from observing the Lord's Day. Traditional activities (sports, restaurants, etc.), and social necessities (public services, etc.), require some people to perform work on Sundays, but everyone should still take care to set aside sufficient time for leisure. With temperance and charity the faithful will see to it that they avoid the excesses and violence sometimes associated with popular leisure activities. In spite of economic constraints, public authorities should ensure citizens a time intended for rest and divine worship. Employers have a similar obligation towards their employees."

—*Catechism of the Catholic Church*, 2187 (528)

"From this follows the obligation of the cessation from work and labor on Sundays and certain holy days. The rest from labor is not to be understood as mere giving way to idleness; much less must it be an occasion for spending money and for vicious indulgence, as many would have it to be; but it should be rest from labor, hallowed by religion. Rest (combined with religious observances) disposes man to forget for a while the business of his everyday life, to turn his thoughts to things heavenly, and to the worship which he so strictly owes to the eternal Godhead. It is this, above all, which is the reason and motive of Sunday rest; a rest sanctioned by God's great law of the Ancient Covenant—'Remember thou keep holy the Sabbath day,' (Ex 20:8) and taught to the world by His own mysterious 'rest' after the creation of man: 'He rested on the seventh day from all His work which He had done.' (Gn 2:2)"

—Leo XIII, *Rerum novarum*, 41

57. Should we make any special allowances for disabled employees?

"Careful attention must be devoted to the physical and psychological working conditions of disabled people—as for all workers—to their just remuneration, to the possibility of their promotion, and to the elimination of various obstacles. Without hiding the fact that this is a complex and difficult task, it is to be hoped that *a correct concept of labor in the subjective sense* will produce a situation which will make it possible for disabled people to feel that they are not cut off from the working world or dependent upon society, but that they are full-scale subjects of work, useful, respected for their human dignity and called to contribute to the progress and welfare of their families and of the community according to their particular capacities."

—St. John Paul II, *Laborem exercens*, 22

58. Does the concept of subsidiarity have any relevance and practical implications for how much authority we delegate to junior staff?

"[The principle of] subsidiarity provides business leaders with three practical steps: (1) Clearly define the realm of autonomy and decision rights to be made at every level in the company, leaving these as wide as possible. Limits should be set such that decision rights do not exceed a person or group's ability to access the information required to make the decision, and so the consequences of the decisions would not overstep their realm of responsibility. (2) Teach and equip employees, making sure that they have the right tools, training, and experience to carry out their tasks. (3) Accept that the persons to whom tasks and responsibilities have been given will make their decisions in freedom, and, thereby in full trust, [accept] the risks of their decisions. Subsidiary business structures should therefore nurture mutual respect and responsibility and allow employees to attribute good results to their sincere engagement."

—Pontifical Council for Justice and Peace, *Vocation of the Business Leader*, 49

"God has not willed to reserve to himself all exercise of power. He entrusts to every creature the functions it is capable of performing, according to the capacities of its own nature. This mode of governance ought to be followed in social life. The way God acts in governing the world, which bears witness to such great regard for human freedom, should inspire the wisdom of those who govern human communities."

—*Catechism of the Catholic Church*, 1884 (460)

"Neither the State nor any society must ever substitute itself for the initiative and responsibility of individuals and of intermediate communities at the level on which they can function, nor must they take away the room necessary for their freedom."

—Congregation for the Doctrine of the Faith, "Instruction on Christian Freedom and Liberation," 73

"In economic enterprises it is persons who are joined together, that is, free and independent human beings created in the image of God. Therefore, with attention to the functions of each—owners or employers, management or labor—and without doing harm to the necessary unity of management, the active sharing of all in the administration and profits of these enterprises in ways to be properly determined is to be promoted."

—*Gaudium et spes*, 68

Labor-Management Relations

59. How ought labor and management to conduct themselves in dealing with each other?

"When we consider a business organization as a community of persons, it becomes clear that the bonds which hold us in common are not merely legal contracts or mutual self-interests, but commitments to real goods, shared with others to serve the world. It is dangerous and misinformed simply to consider business as a 'society of shares,' where self-interests, contracts, utility, and financial profit maximization exhaust its meaning."

—Pontifical Council for Justice and Peace, *The Vocation of the Business Leader*, 58

"However true it may be that man is destined for work and called to it, in the first place work is 'for man' and not man 'for work.' Through this conclusion one rightly comes to recognize the pre-eminence of the subjective meaning of work over the objective one. Given this way of understanding things, and presupposing that different sorts of work that people do can have greater or lesser objective value, let us try nevertheless to show that each sort is judged above all by the measure of the dignity of the subject of work, that is to say the person, the individual who carries it out."

—St. John Paul II, *Laborem exercens*, 6

"We must first of all recall a principle that has always been taught by the Church: *the principle of the priority of labor over capital.* This principle directly concerns the process of production: in this process labor is always a primary *efficient cause,* while capital, the whole collection of means of production, remains a mere *instrument* or instrumental cause. This principle is an evident truth that emerges from the whole of man's historical experience."

—St. John Paul II, *Laborem exercens*, 12

"Labor was separated from capital and set in opposition to it, and capital was set in opposition to labor, as though they were two impersonal forces, two production factors juxtaposed in the same 'economistic' perspective. This way of stating the issue contained a fundamental error, what we can call *the error of economism,* that of considering human labor solely according to its economic purpose."

—St. John Paul II, *Laborem exercens,* 13

"It is therefore very appropriate, or even necessary, that these public authorities and institutions bring the workers into their discussions, and those who represent the rights, demands and aspirations of the workingmen; and not confine their deliberations to those who merely represent the interests of management."

—St. John XXIII, *Mater et magistra,* 99

"The following duties bind the wealthy owner and the employer: not to look upon their workmen as their bondsmen, but to respect in every man his dignity as a person ennobled by Christian character. They are reminded that, according to natural reason and Christian philosophy, working for gain is creditable, not shameful, to a man, since it enables him to earn an honorable livelihood; but to misuse men as though they were things in the pursuit of gain, or to value them solely for their physical powers—that is truly shameful and inhuman."

—Leo XIII, *Rerum novarum,* 20

"We next proceed to make clear the relations of the members one to another, in order that they may live together in concord and go forward prosperously and with good results. The offices and charges of the society should be apportioned for the good of the society itself, and in such mode that difference in degree or standing should not interfere with unanimity and goodwill. It is most important that office bearers be appointed with due prudence and discretion, and each one's charge carefully mapped out, in order that no members may suffer harm. The common funds must be administered with strict honesty, in such a way that a member may receive assistance in proportion to his necessities. The rights and duties of the employers, as compared with the rights and duties of the employed, ought to be the subject of careful consideration. Should it happen that either a master or a workman believes himself injured, nothing would be more desirable than that a committee should be appointed, composed of reliable and capable members of the association, whose duty would be, conformably with the rules of the association, to settle the dispute. Among the several purposes of a society, one should be to try to arrange for a continuous supply of work at all times and seasons; as well as to create a fund out of which the members may be effectually helped in their needs, not only in the cases of accident, but also in sickness, old age, and distress."

—Leo XIII, *Rerum novarum*, 58

60. Do workers have a right to unionize?

"To achieve these goals there is still need for a broad associated workers' movement, directed towards the liberation and promotion of the whole person."

—St. John Paul II, *Centesimus annus*, 43

"All these rights, together with the need for the workers themselves to secure them, give rise to yet another right: *the right of association*, that is to form associations for the purpose of defending the vital interests of those employed in the various professions. These associations are called *labor or trade unions*. The vital interests of the workers are to a certain extent common for all of them; at the same time however each type of work, each profession, has its own specific character which should find a particular reflection in these organizations."

—St. John Paul II, *Laborem exercens*, 20

"Among the basic rights of the human person is to be numbered the right of freely founding unions for working people. These should be able truly to represent them and to contribute to the organizing of economic life in the right way. Included is the right of freely taking part in the activity of these unions without risk of reprisal. Through this orderly participation joined to progressive economic and social formation, all will grow day by day in the awareness of their own function and responsibility, and thus they will be brought to feel that they are comrades in the whole task of economic development and in the attainment of the universal common good according to their capacities and aptitudes."

—*Gaudium et spes*, 68

61. What should be the role of labor unions?

"Catholic social teaching does not hold that unions are no more than a reflection of the 'class' structure of society and that they are a mouthpiece for a class struggle which inevitably governs social life. They are indeed *a mouthpiece for the struggle for social justice*, for the just rights of working people in accordance with their individual professions. However, this struggle should be seen as a normal endeavor 'for' the just good: in the present case, for the good which corresponds to the needs and merits of working people associated by profession; but it is *not a struggle 'against' others*. Even if in controversial questions the struggle takes on a character of opposition towards others, this is because it aims at the good of social justice, not for the sake of 'struggle' or in order to eliminate the opponent."

—St. John Paul II, *Laborem exercens*, 20

"In the task of development man finds the family to be the first and most basic social structure; but he is often helped by professional organizations. While such organizations are founded to aid and assist their members, they bear a heavy responsibility for the task of education which they can and must carry out. In training and developing individual men, they do much to cultivate in them an awareness of the common good and of its demands upon all.

"Every form of social action involves some doctrine; and the Christian rejects that which is based on a materialistic and atheistic philosophy, namely one which shows no respect for a religious outlook on life, for freedom or human dignity. So long as these higher values are preserved intact, however, the existence of a variety of professional organizations and trade unions is permissible. Variety may even help to preserve freedom and create friendly rivalry. We gladly commend those people who unselfishly serve their brothers by working in such organizations."

—Paul VI, *Populorum progressio*, 38–39

"We may lay it down as a general and lasting law that working men's associations should be so organized and governed as to furnish the best and most suitable means for attaining what is aimed at, that is to say, for helping each individual member to better his condition to the utmost in body, soul, and property. It is clear that they must pay special and chief attention to the duties of religion and morality, and that social betterment should have this chiefly in view; otherwise they would lose wholly their special character, and end by becoming little better than those societies which take no account whatever of religion. What advantage can it be to a working man to obtain by means of a society material well-being, if he endangers his soul for lack of spiritual food?"

—Leo XIII, *Rerum novarum*, 57

62. Do workers have a right to strike?

"Recourse to a strike is morally legitimate when it cannot be avoided, or at least when it is necessary to obtain a proportionate benefit. It becomes morally unacceptable when accompanied by violence, or when objectives are included that are not directly linked to working conditions or are contrary to the common good."

—Catechism of the Catholic Church, 2435 (585)

"*One method* used by unions in pursuing the just rights of their members is *the strike* or work stoppage, as a kind of ultimatum to the competent bodies, especially the employers. This method is recognized by Catholic social teaching as legitimate in the proper conditions and within just limits. In this connection workers should be assured the *right to strike*, without being subjected to personal penal sanctions for taking part in a strike. While admitting that it is a legitimate means, we must at the same time emphasize that a strike remains, in a sense, an extreme means. It *must not be abused;* it must not be abused especially for 'political' purposes. Furthermore it must never be forgotten that, when essential community services are in question, they must in every case be ensured, if necessary by means of appropriate legislation. Abuse of the strike weapon can lead to the paralysis of the whole of socioeconomic life, and this is contrary to the requirements of the common good of society, which also corresponds to the properly understood nature of work itself."

—St. John Paul II, *Laborem exercens*, 20

"When, however, socio-economic disputes arise, efforts must be made to come to a peaceful settlement. Although recourse must always be had first to a sincere dialogue between the parties, a strike, nevertheless, can remain even in present day circumstances a necessary, though ultimate, aid for the defense of the workers' own rights and the fulfillment of their just desires. As soon as possible, however, ways should be sought to resume negotiation and the discussion of reconciliation."

—*Gaudium et spes*, 68

Hiring and Firing

63. In hiring decisions, may we discriminate against hiring someone whose immoral behavior outside the workplace will likely be demoralizing to other employees?

"Hence, the employer is bound to see that the worker... be not exposed to corrupting influences and dangerous occasions."

—Leo XIII, *Rerum novarum*, 20

64. Is it morally acceptable to lay off staff solely for the purposes of increasing profits and/or improving the company's share price?

"In the Church's teaching, ownership has never been understood in a way that could constitute grounds for social conflict in labor.... Property is acquired first of all through work in order that it may serve work."

—St. John Paul II, *Laborem exercens*, 14

"This concerns in a special way ownership of the means of production.... They cannot be *possessed against labor,* they cannot even be *possessed for possession's sake,* because the only legitimate title to their possession—whether in the form of private ownership or in the form of public or collective ownership— is *that they should serve labor,* and thus, by serving labor, that they should make possible the achievement of the first principle of this order, namely, the universal destination of goods and the right to common use of them."

—St. John Paul II, *Laborem exercens*, 14

65. Is there anything wrong with laying off people and replacing them with technology, if this will improve product quality and profits?

"The goal should not be that technological progress increasingly replace human work, for this would be detrimental to humanity. Work is a necessity, part of the meaning of life on this earth, a path to growth, human development and personal fulfillment.... the orientation of the economy has favoured a kind of technological progress in which the costs of production are reduced by laying off workers and replacing them with machines. This is yet another way in which we can end up working against ourselves. The loss of jobs also has a negative impact on the economy 'through the progressive erosion of social capital: the network of relationships of trust, dependability, and respect for rules, all of which are indispensable for any form of civil coexistence.' In other words, 'human costs always include economic costs, and economic dysfunctions always involve human costs.' To stop investing in people, in order to gain greater short-term financial gain, is bad business for society."

—Francis, *Laudato Si*, 128 (quoting Benedict XVI, *Caritas in Veritate*, 32

"These new conditions and demands will require a reordering and adjustment of the structures of the modern economy and of the distribution of work. Unfortunately, for millions of skilled workers these changes may perhaps mean unemployment, at least for a time, or the need for retraining. They will very probably involve a reduction or a less rapid increase in material wellbeing for the more developed countries. But they can also bring relief and hope to the millions who today live in conditions of shameful and unworthy poverty.

"It is not for the Church to analyze scientifically the consequences that these changes may have on human society. But the Church considers it her task always to call attention to the dignity and rights of those who work, to condemn situations in which that dignity and those rights are violated, and to help to guide the above-mentioned changes so as to ensure authentic progress by man and society."

—St. John Paul II, *Laborem exercens*, 1

"Understood in this case not as a capacity or aptitude for work, but rather as a *whole set of instruments* which man uses in his work, technology is undoubtedly man's ally. It facilitates his work, perfects, accelerates and augments it. It leads to an increase in the quantity of things produced by work, and in many cases improves their quality. However, it is also a fact that, in some instances, technology can cease to be man's ally and become almost his enemy, as when the mechanization of work 'supplants' him, taking away all personal satisfaction and the incentive to creativity and responsibility, when it deprives many workers of their previous employment, or when, through exalting the machine, it reduces man to the status of its slave."

—St. John Paul II, *Laborem exercens,* 5

— 4 —

Marketing and Sales

Product Portfolio

66. Are there any moral limitations on what we can make
and sell, or should we just let the market decide?

"Needs ought to be contrasted with mere wants, which might
be characterized as satisfying desires which do not contribute
to human well-being. In extreme cases, meeting such desires
may even be detrimental to human well-being as, for example,
in the sale of non-therapeutic drugs, pornography, gambling,
violent video games, and other harmful products."

—Pontifical Council for Justice and Peace, *Vocation of the Business Leader,* 42

"Of itself, an economic system does not possess criteria for correctly distinguishing new and higher forms of satisfying human needs from artificial new needs which hinder the formation of a mature personality. *Thus a great deal of educational
and cultural work* is urgently needed, including the education
of consumers in the responsible use of their power of choice,
the formation of a strong sense of responsibility among pro-

ducers and among people in the mass media in particular, as well as the necessary intervention by public authorities."

—St. John Paul II, *Centesimus annus*, 36

"Here we find a new limit on the market: there are collective and qualitative needs which cannot be satisfied by market mechanisms. There are important human needs which escape its logic. There are goods which by their very nature cannot and must not be bought or sold. Certainly the mechanisms of the market offer secure advantages: they help to utilize resources better; they promote the exchange of products; above all they give central place to the person's desires and preferences, which, in a contract, meet the desires and preferences of another person. Nevertheless, these mechanisms carry the risk of an 'idolatry' of the market, an idolatry which ignores the existence of goods which by their nature are not and cannot be mere commodities."

—St. John Paul II, *Centesimus annus*, 40

67. What criteria should we use to decide what kinds of products and services are morally acceptable?

"Needs ought to be contrasted with mere wants, which might be characterized as satisfying desires which do not contribute to human well-being. In extreme cases, meeting such desires may even be detrimental to human well-being as, for example, in the sale of non-therapeutic drugs, pornography, gambling, violent video games, and other harmful products."

—Pontifical Council for Justice and Peace, *Vocation of the Business Leader*, 42

"Work becomes ever more fruitful and productive to the extent that people become more knowledgeable of the productive potentialities of the earth and more profoundly cognizant of the needs of those for whom their work is done."

—St. John Paul II, *Centesimus annus*, 31

"In singling out new needs and new means to meet them, one must be guided by a comprehensive picture of man which respects all the dimensions of his being and which subordinates his material and instinctive dimensions to his interior and spiritual ones."

—St. John Paul II, *Centesimus annus*, 36

"The fundamental finality of…production is not the mere increase of products nor profit or control but rather the service of man, and indeed of the whole man with regard for the full range of his material needs and the demands of his intellectual, moral, spiritual, and religious life."

—*Gaudium et spes*, 64

68. Is it morally acceptable to be involved in the production or marketing of toys, video games, or movies that glorify violence or sexual promiscuity?

"Any trend to produce programs and products—including animated films and video games—which in the name of entertainment exalt violence and portray anti-social behavior or the trivialization of human sexuality is a perversion, all the more repulsive when these programs are directed at children and adolescents. How could one explain this 'entertainment' to the countless innocent young people who actually suffer violence, exploitation and abuse?"

—Benedict XVI, message for World Communications Day 2007, 3

"Do not corrupt society, and in particular youth, by the approving and insistent depiction of evil, of violence, of moral abjection, carrying out a work of ideological manipulation, sowing discord!"

—St. John Paul II, message for World Communications Day 1984, 4

"Nor can we fail, in the name of the respect due to the human person, to condemn the widespread hedonistic and commercial culture which encourages the systematic exploitation of sexuality and corrupts even very young girls into letting their bodies be used for profit."

—St. John Paul II, "Letter to Women," 5

69. Is it morally acceptable to be involved in the production or marketing of tobacco products?

"While conceding that the Church does not have direct authority in the question of tobacco, We alluded to some reserves. Did We, then, have in view one particular aspect, where she would have her word to say, an aspect of the moral order, evidently? To be precise, it is two-fold.

"1. It is necessary, in conscience, when manipulating tobacco, to eliminate, insofar as possible, the toxic elements. In the first place it concerns you: the poisonings and other accidents which too often affect the general health or the organs of smokers, should be reduced to the minimum, and it is for all those who take part in its handling a duty of conscience; it is thus necessary that each one in his sphere contribute to his task all the competence and all the care desirable....

"2. Each one should employ tobacco with moderation and taking into account numerous factors which have to enter in, in order to make of this use a sanely moral act.

"We spoke of another moral aspect of the question of tobacco where the solicitude of the Church has a place to be shown. This is of a general nature: We wish to say the duty common to all of watching over the regulation of the use of tobacco in such a way that it is in accord with physical and moral health, with economic possibilities, with the social obligations of individuals and peoples."

—Pius XII, address to members of the Conference of the European Tobacco Center (September 14, 1950); quoted in Robert Kennedy and Stephanie Rumpza, eds., *Pius XII: On Work and Commerce*, http://www.stthomas.edu/cathstudies/cst/publications/PiusXII.html

70. Is it morally acceptable to be involved in the gambling industry?

"Games of chance (card games, etc.) or wagers are not in themselves contrary to justice. They become morally unacceptable when they deprive someone of what is necessary to provide for his needs and those of others. The passion for gambling risks becoming an enslavement. Unfair wagers and cheating at games constitute grave matter, unless the damage inflicted is so slight that the one who suffers it cannot reasonably consider it significant."

—*Catechism of the Catholic Church*, 2413 (580)

71. Is it morally acceptable to be involved in the production or marketing of birth control products?

"A civilization inspired by a consumerist, anti-birth mentality is not and cannot ever be a civilization of love."

—St. John Paul II, "Letter to Families," 13

"An act of mutual love which impairs the capacity to transmit life which God the Creator, through specific laws, has built into it, frustrates His design which constitutes the norm of marriage, and contradicts the will of the Author of life. Hence to use this divine gift while depriving it, even if only partially, of its meaning and purpose, is equally repugnant to the nature of man and of woman, and is consequently in opposition to the plan of God and His holy will."

—Paul VI, *Humanae vitae*, 13

"Similarly excluded is any action which either before, at the moment of, or after sexual intercourse, is specifically intended to prevent procreation—whether as an end or as a means."

—Paul VI, *Humanae vitae*, 14

72. Is it morally acceptable to be involved in the abortion industry, either directly, or indirectly as a supplier?

"How can we genuinely teach the importance of concern for other vulnerable beings, however troublesome or inconvenient they may be, if we fail to protect a human embryo, even when its presence is uncomfortable and creates difficulties? 'If personal and social sensitivity towards the acceptance of the new life is lost, then other forms of acceptance that are valuable for society also wither away.'"

—Francis, *Laudato Si*, 120 (quoting Benedict XVI, *Caritas in Veritate*, 28)

"[The Church's] defense of unborn life is closely linked to the defense of each and every other human right. It involves the conviction that a human being is always sacred and inviolable, in any situation and at every stage of development. Human beings are ends in themselves and never a means of resolving other problems. Once this conviction disappears, so do solid and lasting foundations for the defense of human rights, which would always be subject to the passing whims of the powers that be. Reason alone is sufficient to recognize the inviolable value of each single human life, but if we also look at the issue from the standpoint of faith, 'every violation of the personal dignity of the human being cries out in vengeance to God and is an offence against the creator of the individual.'"

—Francis, *Evangelii Gaudium*, 213 (quoting St. John Paul II, *Christifideles Laici*, 37)

"Material cooperation can sometimes be illicit …, but when immediate material cooperation concerns grave attacks on human life, it is always to be considered illicit, given the precious nature of the value in question."

—Pontifical Academy for Life, "Moral Reflections on Vaccines Prepared from Cells Derived from Aborted Human Foetuses (June 5, 2005)

"It is never licit to cooperate formally in evil. Such cooperation occurs when an action, either by its very nature or by the form it takes in a concrete situation, can be defined as a direct participation in an act against innocent human life or a sharing in the immoral intention of the person committing it."

—St. John Paul II, *Evangelium vitae*, 74

"The direct interruption of the generative process already begun and, above all, all direct abortion, even for therapeutic reasons, are to be absolutely excluded as lawful means of regulating the number of children."

—Paul VI, *Humanae vitae*, 14

73. Is it morally acceptable to be involved in the production or marketing of defense equipment?

"The production and sale of arms affect the common good of nations and of the international community. Hence public authorities have the right and duty to regulate them. The short-term pursuit of private or collective interests cannot legitimate undertakings that promote violence and conflict among nations and compromise the international juridical order."

—*Catechism of the Catholic Church,* 2316 (557)

Advertising and Promotion

74. Does Church teaching have relevance to advertising?

"In today's society, advertising has a profound impact on how people understand life, the world and themselves, especially in regard to their values and their ways of choosing and behaving. These are matters about which the Church is and must be deeply and sincerely concerned."

—Pontifical Council for Social Communications, "Ethics in Advertising," 1

"It may be asked why advertising and its bearing upon the instruments of social communication should be of interest to the Church. The answer is that advertising is quite an important element in the common life of man, because it conditions his integral development and, directly or indirectly, has an influence upon his cultural life. No one now can escape the influence of advertising, and, even apart from the actual content of its messages, it presents, at least suggests particular visions of the world, which inevitably pull at the Christian, affect his judgment, and influence his manner of acting. Advertising, more-over, takes on an ever growing importance, because in large part it finances the development of the communications me-dia and uses them for its own purposes, directly and sometimes dangerously influencing their orientation and their freedom."

—Paul VI, message for World Social Communications Day 1977

75. Why are we responsible for our advertising—doesn't it just mirror societal values?

"We disagree with the assertion that advertising simply mirrors the attitudes and values of the surrounding culture. No doubt advertising, like the media of social communications in gen-eral, does act as a mirror. But, also like media in general, it is a mirror that helps shape the reality it reflects, and sometimes it presents a distorted image of reality."

—Pontifical Council for Social Communications, "Ethics in Advertising," 3

76. Is it morally acceptable in advertising to try to "create needs": to appeal directly to consumers' instincts?

"Sometimes advertisers speak of it as part of their task to 'cre-ate' needs for products and services—that is, to cause people to feel and act upon cravings for items and services they do not need. 'If…a direct appeal is made to [the customer's] in-stincts—while ignoring in various ways the reality of the per-son as intelligent and free—then consumer attitudes and life-styles can be created which are objectively improper and often damaging to his physical and spiritual health.'

"This is a serious abuse, an affront to human dignity and the common good when it occurs in affluent societies. But the abuse is still more grave when consumerist attitudes and values are transmitted by communications media and advertising to developing countries, where they exacerbate socio-economic problems and harm the poor."

—Pontifical Council for Social Communications, "Ethics in Advertising," 10 (citing St. John Paul II, *Centesimus annus*, 36)

"We must not omit to mention those crafty men who, wholly unconcerned about any honest usefulness of their work, do not scruple to stimulate the baser human desires and, when they are aroused, use them for their own profit."

—Pius XI, *Quadragesimo anno*, 132

77. Is it morally acceptable to use our advertising to attempt to make people feel inadequate if they don't buy our product?

"*Obedience to the truth* about God and man is the first condition of freedom, making it possible for a person to order his needs and desires and to choose the means of satisfying them according to a correct scale of values, so that the ownership of things may become an occasion of growth for him. This growth can be hindered as a result of manipulation by the means of mass communication, which impose fashions and trends of opinion through carefully orchestrated repetition, without it being possible to subject to critical scrutiny the premises on which these fashions and trends are based."

—St. John Paul II, *Centesimus annus*, 41

"Even a psychological suggestion—apparently harmless—can, when skillfully handled with the tools of persuasion, make a man a target and endanger his freedom. This is the sense in which I mean to speak of social communications as the servant of responsible human freedom. Man is created free. But he is of the kind that must grow and develop by overcoming the self. Freedom has to be won. So a man must free himself from everything that might disqualify him from winning freedom."

—St. John Paul II, message for World Communications Day 1981, 2

78. How can we use advertising in a morally acceptable way?

"Advertising can play an important role in the process by which an economic system guided by moral norms and responsive to the common good contributes to human development. It is a necessary part of the functioning of modern market economies, which today either exist or are emerging in many parts of the world and which—provided they conform to moral standards based upon integral human development and the common good—currently seem to be 'the most efficient instrument for utilizing resources and effectively responding to needs' of a socio-economic kind.

"In such a system, advertising can be a useful tool for sustaining honest and ethically responsible competition that contributes to economic growth in the service of authentic human development."

—Pontifical Council for Social Communications, "Ethics in Advertising," 5
(citing St. John Paul II, *Centesimus annus,* 34)

"The media of social communications have two options, and only two. Either they help human persons to grow in their understanding and practice of what is true and good, or they are destructive forces in conflict with human well being. That is entirely true of advertising."

—Pontifical Council for Social Communications, "Ethics in Advertising," 14

"To remind the communicators that their employment demands from them love, justice, truth, as well as freedom—this is a duty of my pastoral ministry. Truth must never be distorted, justice neglected, love forgotten, if one is to observe ethical standards. To forget or lose sight of these is to produce bias, scandal, submission to the powerful, compliance with 'reasons of state.'"

—St. John Paul II, message for World Communications Day 1981

"The Church looks with favor on the growth of man's productive capacity, and also on the ever widening network of relationships and exchanges between persons and social groups; they are for her a reason, a sign and an anticipation of an ever greater brotherhood, and from this point of view she encourages advertising, which can become a wholesome and efficacious instrument for reciprocal help among men. Another fundamental aspect which the Church recognizes in advertising is its informative aspect, with all the weight and the obligations deriving from it. It has to be truthful, prudent, respectful of man and of his essential values, careful in its choice of the circumstances in which it addresses him, and of the manner in which it makes its presentation.

"Advertising is, then, a promotional tool of particular interests which, even if legitimate, must take the common good into account, keep in mind the equally legitimate interests of others, and especially have due regard for the concrete circumstances of the integral development affecting the people to whom it addresses itself, for their cultural and economic environment, and for the level of education they have attained. As is well known, the advertising message is, naturally, designed to convince people, it makes use of techniques based on precise psychological and social knowledge, and it is constantly researching the ways and means of persuasion. It is here, above all that there is imposed on it and, therefore, on those within the advertising profession, the imperative requirement to respect the human person, his right-duty to make a responsible choice, his interior freedom; all these goods would be violated if man's lower inclinations were to be exploited, or his capacity to reflect and decide compromised."

—Paul VI, message for World Communications Day 1977

"The communicators must, in their turn, know and respect the needs of the family. This presupposes at times much courage on their part, and always a high sense of responsibility. It means in practice, that they should exclude on the one side all that can damage the family in its existence, its stability, its order and its happiness, for every attack on the true fundamental values of the family—whether it be eroticism or violence, the defense of divorce or antisocial attitudes among young people—is an attack on genuine human welfare and the good of society. On the other hand, communicators have the difficult task of educating the public to know, appreciate and love values that are often unknown or despised but which are the strength and the glory of a given society: such as, the dedication of one's self to a great ideal, the sense of sacrifice and the hidden heroism of daily routine."

—Paul VI, message for World Social Communications Day 1969

"For the proper use of these media it is most necessary that all who employ them be acquainted with the norms of morality and conscientiously put them into practice in this area. They must look, then, to the nature of what is communicated, given the special character of each of these media. At the same time they must take into consideration the entire situation or circumstances, namely, the persons, place, time and other conditions under which communication takes place and which can affect or totally change its propriety. Among these circumstances to be considered is the precise manner in which a given medium achieves its effect. For its influence can be so great that men, especially if they are unprepared, can scarcely become aware of it, govern its impact, or, if necessary, reject it."

—Paul VI, *Inter mirifica*, 4, 1963

79. Is it morally acceptable to advertise children's products directly to children?

"To be sure, there is a great richness and vitality in a child's heart; however, he is not capable, all by himself, of resolving the diverse mysteries and longings that assail him from within. It is on the adults that the duty falls—on the parents, the educators, the communications workers—and it is they also who have the capability of enabling the child to sort things out and find himself."

—St. John Paul II, message for World Communications Day 1979

"We witness young people and children, used as easily-secured consumers by an industry that makes itself its own end, being dragged into the pit-falls of eroticism and violence or led along the perilous paths of incertitude, anxiety and anguish. It is not asking too much that all right thinking persons should unite at last to sound a cry of alarm and to put an end to enterprises that deserve to be called corrupting."

—Paul VI, message for World Social Communications Day 1970

"The Church, a tender mother, is not alone in fearing for the welfare of youths. In some countries the new generations from their adolescence and even from infancy suffer from weakness; physical and spiritual anemia caused by material poverty with all its attendant miseries, from an insufficient family life or even from its complete absence, from lack of education and instruction or finally, perhaps, from long years of imprisonment or exile. Among peoples living under better conditions, dangers of another kind—often arising from an excess of wealth and pleasure—menace the physical and moral health of youth. This state is still sadder."

—Pius XII, address to the College of Cardinals on the feast of St. Eugene (June 2, 1947)[1]

80. Is it morally acceptable to use advertising to persuade teenagers that they will not be "cool" unless they use our product, particularly if this technique is proving to be very successful for our competitors?

"We point to this fundamental principle for people engaged in advertising: advertisers—that is, those who commission, prepare or disseminate advertising—are morally responsible for what they seek to move people to do; and this is a responsibility also shared by publishers, broadcasting executives, and others in the communications world, as well as by those who give commercial or political endorsements, to the extent that they are involved in the advertising process."

—Pontifical Council for Social Communications, "Ethics in Advertising," 14

81. Is it morally acceptable to use any kind of sexual imagery or innuendo in our advertising, particularly if we are in an industry (e.g., underwear, high fashion products, beer) where most or all of our competitors do so, and it seems to be required for success?

"There is a modesty of the feelings as well as of the body. It protests, for example, against the voyeuristic explorations of the

1. *The Catholic Mind,* August 1947, 440–57.

human body in certain advertisements, or against the solici-
tations of certain media that go too far in the exhibition of
intimate things. Modesty inspires a way of life which makes it
possible to resist the allurements of fashion and the pressures
of prevailing ideologies."

—*Catechism of the Catholic Church*, 2523 (604)

"It is not so easy to resist commercial pressures or the demands
of conformity to secular ideologies, but that is what responsible communicators must do. The stakes are high, since every
attack on the fundamental value of the family is an attack on
the true good of humanity."

—St. John Paul II, message for World Communications Day 2004

"There is then the danger to the responsible freedom of those
who use the means of social communications, a danger which
takes the form of a serious attack and is marked by the use of
sex to the point where there is an outbreak of pornography:
in the spoken or written word, in pictures and even so-called
'artistic' posters. At times this is tantamount to pandering, the
result of which is both destructive and perverting. The denunciation of this state of affairs does not mean displaying what is
so often described as 'reactionary mentality' or censorship of
free-will: the denunciation is done in the very name of freedom, which demands and necessitates that one does not suffer
the imposition of those who seek to transform sexuality into
an end in itself. This action would be not only anti-Christian
but anti-human, with the consequent transition to drugs, perversion and degeneration."

—St. John Paul II, message for World Communications Day 1981

"Everything therefore in the modern means of social communication which arouses men's baser passions and encourages low

moral standards, as well as every obscenity in the written word and every form of indecency on the stage and screen, should be condemned publicly and unanimously by all those who have at heart the advance of civilization and the safeguarding of the outstanding values of the human spirit. It is quite absurd to defend this kind of depravity in the name of art or culture or by pleading the liberty which may be allowed in this field by the public authorities."

—Paul VI, *Humanae vitae*, 22

"Some have become so hardened to the stings of conscience as to hold that they are allowed, in any manner whatsoever, to increase their profits and use means, fair or foul, to protect their hard-won wealth against sudden changes of fortune...[including] those crafty men who, wholly unconcerned about any honest usefulness of their work, do not scruple to stimulate the baser human desires and, when they are aroused, use them for their own profit."

—Pius XI, *Quadragesimo anno*, 132

82. Is it morally acceptable to use imagery to differentiate between two competing brands that are functionally equivalent (e.g., colas, toothpastes, washing powders)?

"The practice of 'brand'-related advertising can raise serious problems. Often there are only negligible differences among similar products of different brands, and advertising may attempt to move people to act on the basis of irrational motives ('brand loyalty,' status, fashion, 'sex appeal,' etc.) instead of presenting differences in product quality and price as bases for rational choice."

—Pontifical Council for Social Communications, "Ethics in Advertising," 10

83. Is it morally acceptable to use members of the clergy or religious imagery to sell products?

"We note, too, certain special problems relating to advertising that treats of religion or pertains to specific issues with a moral dimension.... Commercial advertisers sometimes include religious themes or use religious images or personages to sell products. It is possible to do this in tasteful, acceptable ways, but the practice is obnoxious and offensive when it involves exploiting religion or treating it flippantly."

—Pontifical Council for Social Communications, "Ethics in Advertising," 13

"They should see to it that communications or presentations concerning religious matters are entrusted to worthy and experienced hands and are carried out with fitting reverence."

—Paul VI, *Inter mirifica*, 11 1963

84. Is it morally acceptable to be involved in the promotion of harmless but wasteful or trivial products, if people seem to be willing to buy them?

"In a world tempted by consumerist and materialist outlooks, Christian executives are called to affirm the priority of 'being' over 'having.'"

—St. John Paul II, message to participants in the conference "The Business Executive: Social Responsibility and Globalization" (March 3, 2004)

"If harmful or utterly useless goods are touted to the public, if false assertions are made about the goods for sale, if less admirable human tendencies are exploited, those responsible for such advertising harm society and forfeit their good name and credibility. More than this, unremitting pressure to buy articles of luxury can arouse false wants that hurt both individuals and families by making them ignore what they really need."

—*Communio et progressio, 60*

85. Is it morally wrong to contribute to a culture of consumerism?

"In economic matters, respect for human dignity requires the practice of the virtue of temperance, so as to moderate our attachment to this world's goods."

—*Catechism of the Catholic Church, 2407 (578)*

"[Promotion of consumerism] is a serious abuse, an affront to human dignity and the common good when it occurs in affluent societies. But the abuse is still more grave when consumerist attitudes and values are transmitted by communications media and advertising to developing countries, where they exacerbate socio-economic problems and harm the poor."

—*Pontifical Council for Social Communications, "Ethics in Advertising," 10*

"Advertising that fosters a lavish life style which wastes resources and despoils the environment offends against important ecological concerns. 'In his desire to have and to enjoy rather than to be and grow, man consumes the resources of the earth and his own life in an excessive and disordered way....Man thinks that he can make arbitrary use of the earth, subjecting it without restraint to his will, as though it did not have its own requisites and a prior God-given purpose, which man can indeed develop but must not betray.'

"As this suggests, something more fundamental is at issue here: authentic and integral human development. Advertising that reduces human progress to acquiring material goods and cultivating a lavish life style expresses a false, destructive vision of the human person harmful to individuals and society alike.

"When people fail to practice 'a rigorous respect for the moral, cultural and spiritual requirements, based on the dignity of the person and on the proper identity of each community, beginning with the family and religious societies,' then even material abundance and the conveniences that technology makes available 'will prove unsatisfying and in the end contemptible.' Advertisers, like people engaged in other forms of social communication, have a serious duty to express and foster an authentic vision of human development in its material, cultural and spiritual dimensions. Communication that meets this standard is, among other things, a true expression of solidarity. Indeed, the two things—communication and solidarity—are inseparable, because, as the *Catechism of the Catholic Church* points out, solidarity is 'a consequence of genuine and right communication and the free circulation of ideas that further knowledge and respect for others.'"

> —Pontifical Council for Social Communications, "Ethics in Advertising," 17 (quoting St. John Paul II, *Centesimus annus*, 37 and *Sollicitudo rei socialis*, 33, and the *Catechism of the Catholic Church*, 2495 [598])

"It is not wrong to want to live better; what is wrong is a style of life which is presumed to be better when it is directed towards 'having' rather than 'being,' and which wants to have more, not in order to be more but in order to spend life in enjoyment as an end in itself. It is therefore necessary to create life-styles in which the quest for truth, beauty, goodness and communion with others for the sake of common growth are the factors which determine consumer choices, savings and investments."

> —St. John Paul II, *Centesimus annus*, 36

"This super-development, which consists in an excessive availability of every kind of material goods for the benefit of certain social groups, easily makes people slaves of 'possession' and of immediate gratification, with no other horizon than the multiplication or continual replacement of the things already owned with others still better. This is the so-called civilization of 'consumption' or 'consumerism,' which involves so much 'throwing-away' and 'waste.' An object already owned but now superseded by something better is discarded, with no thought of its possible lasting value in itself, nor of some other human being who is poorer."

—St. John Paul II, *Sollicitudo rei socialis*, 28

"Neither individuals nor nations should regard the possession of more and more goods as the ultimate objective. Every kind of progress is a two-edged sword. It is necessary if man is to grow as a human being; yet it can also enslave him, if he comes to regard it as the supreme good and cannot look beyond it. When this happens, men harden their hearts, shut out others from their minds and gather together solely for reasons of self-interest rather than out of friendship; dissension and disunity follow soon after. Thus the exclusive pursuit of material possessions prevents man's growth as a human being and stands in opposition to his true grandeur. Avarice, in individuals and in nations, is the most obvious form of stultified moral development."

—Paul VI, *Populorum progressio*, 19

86. Is there any particular moral sensitivity we should have when advertising in developing countries?

"Advertising also can have a corrupting influence upon culture and cultural values. We have spoken of the economic harm

that can be done to developing nations by advertising that
fosters consumerism and destructive patterns of consumption. Consider also the cultural injury done to these nations
and their peoples by advertising whose content and methods,
reflecting those prevalent in the first world, are at war with
sound traditional values in indigenous cultures."

—Pontifical Council for Social Communications, "Ethics in Advertising," 12

Pricing

87. What is a just price, and do we have any moral
obligation to offer goods at a just price?

"Even if it does not contradict the provisions of civil law, any
form of unjustly taking and keeping the property of others is
against the seventh commandment: [e.g.]...forcing up prices by taking advantage of the ignorance or hardship of another." [footnote reference to Dt 25:13–16, 24:14–15; Jas 5:4;
Am 8:4–6]

—Catechism of the Catholic Church, 2409 (579)

"A person who produces something other than for his own
use generally does so in order that others may use it after they
have paid a just price, mutually agreed upon through free bar-
gaining."

—St. John Paul II, Centesimus annus, 32

"Let not compassion be forgotten when large firms establish
prices for their medicines; for as far as is in his power, man
must love his fellow man."

—Pius XII, discourse to participants in the International Congress of
the History of Pharmacy, "Pharmacy: An Ancient and Modern Art"
(September 11, 1954)

"But if the business in question is not making enough money to pay the workers an equitable wage because it is being crushed by unjust burdens or forced to sell its product at less than a just price, those who are thus the cause of the injury are guilty of grave wrong, for they deprive workers of their just wage and force them under the pinch of necessity to accept a wage less than fair."

—Pius XI, *Quadragesimo anno*, 72

88. May larger enterprises use their size to gain advantage over other businesses (e.g., through pricing practices)?

"Economies of scale, especially in the agricultural sector, end up forcing smallholders to sell their land or to abandon their traditional crops. Their attempts to move to other, more diversified, means of production prove fruitless because of the difficulty of linkage with regional and global markets, or because the infrastructure for sales and transport is geared to larger businesses."

—Francis, *Laudato Si*, 129

"'The small and average sized undertakings in agriculture, in the arts and crafts, in commerce and industry, should be safeguarded and fostered. Moreover, they should join together in co-operative associations to gain for themselves the benefits and advantages that usually can be gained only from large organizations.'"

—St. John XXIII, *Mater et magistra,* 84 (quoting Pius XII, broadcast message, September 1, 1944)

Sales

89. Is bluffing in negotiation morally acceptable, either to defend our position or to get a better deal?

"The substantial novelty brought by Jesus is that he opened the way to a more human and freer world, with full respect for the distinction and autonomy that exists between what belongs to Caesar and what belongs to God (cf. Mt 22:21). If, therefore, on the one hand, the Church recognizes that she is not and does not intend to be a political agent, on the other, she cannot avoid concerning herself with the good of the whole civil community in which she lives and works and to which she makes her own special contribution, shaping in the political and entrepreneurial classes a genuine spirit of truth and honesty geared to seeking the common good rather than personal advantage."

—Benedict XVI, letter to the president of the Italian Bishops' Conference on the occasion of the centenary of the Italian Catholic Social Week (October 12, 2007)

"All contracts must be agreed to and executed in good faith."

—*Catechism of the Catholic Church,* 2410 (579)

"Truth must never be distorted, justice neglected, love forgotten, if one is to observe ethical standards."

—St. John Paul II, message for World Communications Day 1981, 3

90. May we sell our products or services to an organization that we believe will put them to an immoral use, e.g., printing services to a company that produces pornographic magazines?

See the section "Moral Dilemmas in Business" in chapter 1.

91. May we sell any product or service to an organization that has intrinsically evil ends, e.g., printing services to an abortion clinic?

"Material cooperation can sometimes be illicit …, but when immediate material cooperation concerns grave attacks on human life, it is always to be considered illicit, given the precious nature of the value in question."

—Pontifical Academy for Life, "Moral Reflections on Vaccines Prepared from Cells Derived from Aborted Human Foetuses" (June 5, 2005)

"It is never licit to cooperate formally in evil. Such cooperation occurs when an action, either by its very nature or by the form it takes in a concrete situation, can be defined as a direct participation in an act against innocent human life or a sharing in the immoral intention of the person committing it."

—St. John Paul II, *Evangelium vitae*, 74

92. Is it wrong to target our products and services to certain groups of poorer or more vulnerable customers, where their relatively lower sophistication, lower education levels, and perhaps inability to get credit make them "captive," and therefore more profitable, customers for us?

"The Christian business leader is alert for opportunities to serve…otherwise underserved populations and sees this not only as a proper social responsibility but also as a great business opportunity. Developments in the field of the 'bottom of the pyramid' products and services—such as microenterprises, microcredit, social enterprises, and social investment funds—have played an important role in addressing the needs of the poor. These innovations will not only help lift people from extreme poverty but could spark their own creativity and entrepreneurship and contribute to launching a dynamic of development."

—Pontifical Council for Justice and Peace, *Vocation of the Business Leader*, 43

"Even if it does not contradict the provisions of civil law, any form of unjustly taking and keeping the property of others is against the seventh commandment: [e.g.]...forcing up prices by taking advantage of the ignorance or hardship of another." [footnote reference to Dt 25:13–16, 24:14–15; Jas 5:4; Am 8:4–6]

—*Catechism of the Catholic Church*, 2409 (579)

−5−

Manufacturing

93. Are there any moral obligations regarding what level of quality to maintain in the goods that we produce?

"The following [is] also morally illicit:...work poorly done."

—*Catechism of the Catholic Church*, 2409 (579)

94. Are there any moral obligations regarding a firm's treatment of the environment, beyond following the law?

"The destruction of the human environment is extremely serious, not only because God has entrusted the world to us men and women, but because human life is itself a gift which must be defended from various forms of debasement."

—Francis, *Laudato Si*, 5

"Each community can take from the bounty of the earth whatever it needs for subsistence, but it also has the duty to protect the earth and to ensure its fruitfulness for coming generations."

—Francis, *Laudato Si*, 67

"Environmental impact assessment should not come after the drawing up of a business proposition or the proposal of a particular policy, plan or programme. It should be part of the process from the beginning, and be carried out in a way which is interdisciplinary, transparent and free of all economic or political pressure. It should be linked to a study of working conditions and possible effects on people's physical and mental health, on the local economy and on public safety."

—Francis, *Laudato Si*, 183

"In any discussion about a proposed venture, a number of questions need to be asked in order to discern whether or not it will contribute to genuine integral development. What will it accomplish? Why? Where? When? How? For whom? What are the risks? What are the costs? Who will pay those costs and how? In this discernment, some questions must have higher priority. For example, we know that water is a scarce and indispensable resource and a fundamental right which conditions the exercise of other human rights. This indisputable fact overrides any other assessment of environmental impact on a region."

—Francis, *Laudato Si*, 185

"Man thinks that he can make arbitrary use of the earth, subjecting it without restraint to his will, as though it did not have its own requisites and a prior God-given purpose, which man can indeed develop but must not betray. Instead of carrying out his role as a co-operator with God in the work of creation, man sets himself up in place of God and thus ends up provoking a rebellion on the part of nature, which is more tyrannized than governed by him."

—St. John Paul II, *Centesimus annus*, 37

"The seventh commandment enjoins respect for the integrity of creation. Animals, like plants and inanimate beings, are by nature destined for the common good of past, present, and future humanity. [footnote reference to Gn 1:28–31] Use of the mineral, vegetable, and animal resources of the universe cannot be divorced from respect for moral imperatives. Man's dominion over inanimate and other living beings granted by the Creator is not absolute; it is limited by concern for the quality of life of his neighbor, including generations to come; it requires a religious respect for the integrity of creation." [footnote reference to *Centesimus annus* 37–38]

— Catechism of the Catholic Church, 2415 (580)

"In God's plan man and woman have the vocation of 'subduing' the earth [footnote reference to Gn 1:28] as stewards of God. This sovereignty is not to be an arbitrary and destructive domination. God calls man and woman, made in the image of the Creator 'who loves everything that exists,' [footnote reference to Wis 11:24] to share in his providence toward other creatures; hence their responsibility for the world God has entrusted them."

— Catechism of the Catholic Church, 373 (95)

"The family needs a home, a fit environment in which to develop its proper relationships. *For the human family, this home is the earth,* the environment that God the Creator has given us to inhabit with creativity and responsibility. We need to care for the environment: it has been entrusted to men and women to be protected and cultivated with responsible freedom, with the good of all as a constant guiding criterion."

— Benedict XVI, message for the World Day of Peace 2008, 7

95. Is it morally acceptable to invest in technology that improves our treatment of the environment, if this is not required by law, does not improve our market position, and reduces the profits that would otherwise go to the firm's owners?

"Human beings, obviously, are of supreme worth vis-à-vis creation as a whole. Respecting the environment does not mean considering material or animal nature more important than man. Rather, it means not selfishly considering nature to be at the complete disposal of our own interests, for future generations also have the right to reap its benefits and to exhibit towards nature the same responsible freedom that we claim for ourselves. Nor must we overlook the poor, who are excluded in many cases from the goods of creation destined for all. Humanity today is rightly concerned about the ecological balance of tomorrow. It is important for assessments in this regard to be carried out prudently, in dialogue with experts and people of wisdom, uninhibited by ideological pressure to draw hasty conclusions, and above all with the aim of reaching agreement on a model of sustainable development capable of ensuring the well-being of all while respecting environmental balances. If the protection of the environment involves costs, they should be justly distributed, taking due account of the different levels of development of various countries and the need for solidarity with future generations. Prudence does not mean failing to accept responsibilities and postponing decisions; it means being committed to making joint decisions after pondering responsibly the road to be taken, decisions aimed at strengthening that covenant between human beings and the environment, which should mirror the creative love of God, from whom we come and towards whom we are journeying."

—Benedict XVI, message for the World Day of Peace 2008, 7

"All people of good will must work to ensure the effective protection of the environment, understood as a gift from God."

—St. John Paul II, *Ecclesia in America*, 25

"As one called to till and look after the garden of the world (cf. Gn 2:15), man has a specific responsibility towards the environment in which he lives, towards the creation which God has put at the service of his personal dignity, of his life, not only for the present but also for future generations. It is the ecological question—ranging from the preservation of the natural habitats of the different species of animals and of other forms of life to 'human ecology' properly speaking—which finds in the Bible clear and strong ethical direction, leading to a solution which respects the great good of life, of every life. In fact, 'the dominion granted to man by the Creator is not an absolute power, nor can one speak of a freedom to "use and misuse," or to dispose of things as one pleases. The limitation imposed from the beginning by the Creator himself and expressed symbolically by the prohibition not to "eat of the fruit of the tree" (cf. Gn 2:16–17) shows clearly enough that, when it comes to the natural world, we are subject not only to biological laws but also to moral ones, which cannot be violated with impunity.'"

—St. John Paul II, *Evangelium vitae*, 42 (quoting *Sollicitudo rei socialis*, 34)

"[Creating the conditions for worldwide development] may mean making important changes in established life-styles, in order to limit the waste of environmental and human resources, thus enabling every individual and all the peoples of the earth to have a sufficient share of those resources."

—St. John Paul II, *Centesimus annus*, 52

96. Is it morally acceptable to use animals for food, clothing, or work?

"God entrusted animals to the stewardship of those whom he created in his own image. [footnote reference to Gn 2:19–20; 9:1–4] Hence it is legitimate to use animals for food and clothing. They may be domesticated to help man in his work and leisure."

—*Catechism of the Catholic Church,* 2417 (581)

97. Should food manufacturers have any concern about how animals are treated, beyond what is required by law (e.g., is breeding animals in close confinement acceptable)?

"The first consideration is the appropriateness of acquiring a growing awareness of the fact that one cannot use with impunity the different categories of beings, whether living or inanimate—animals, plants, the natural elements—simply as one wishes, according to one's own economic needs. On the contrary, one must take into account the nature of each being and of its mutual connection in an ordered system, which is precisely the cosmos."

—St. John Paul II, *Sollicitudo rei socialis,* 34

"It is contrary to human dignity to cause animals to suffer needlessly."

—*Catechism of the Catholic Church,* 2418 (581)

98. Is using animals for testing products morally acceptable?

"Medical and scientific experimentation on animals is a morally acceptable practice, if it remains within reasonable limits and contributes to caring for or saving human lives."

—*Catechism of the Catholic Church,* 2417 (581)

– 6 –

International Business

99. Is it morally acceptable to pay large tips, or bribes, in cultures where these appear to be required for conducting business transactions?

"The following [is] also morally illicit:...corruption in which one influences the judgment of those who must make decisions according to law."

—*Catechism of the Catholic Church*, 2409 (579)

100. May we subcontract our manufacturing to offshore manufacturers if there is some concern that they use child labor and/or maintain unsafe conditions for their workers?

"The responsibility of the indirect employer differs from that of the direct employer...but it remains a true responsibility: the indirect employer substantially determines one or other facet of the labor relationship, thus conditioning the conduct of the direct employer when the latter determines in concrete terms the actual work contract and labor relations....

"The attainment of the worker's rights cannot however be deemed to be merely a result of economic systems which on a larger or smaller scale are guided chiefly by the criterion of maximum profit. On the contrary, it is respect for the objective rights of the worker—every kind of worker: manual or intellectual, industrial or agricultural, etc.—that must constitute *the adequate and fundamental criterion* for shaping the whole economy, both on the level of the individual society and State and within the whole of the world economic policy and of the systems of international relationships that derive from it."

—St. John Paul II, *Laborem exercens*, 17

101. What should we do if the only way to remain competitive is to subcontract our manufacturing offshore to contractors who are known to provide unsafe conditions for their workers?

"The responsibility of the indirect employer differs from that of the direct employer…but it remains a true responsibility."

—St. John Paul II, *Laborem exercens*, 17

"There should never be overlooked the right to a working environment and to manufacturing processes which are not harmful to the workers' physical health or to their moral integrity."

—St. John Paul II, *Laborem exercens*, 19

102. To what extent should we focus our efforts on improving the lot of the workers we employ in developing countries, if this comes at the expense of our profits?

"Goods of production—material or immaterial—such as land, factories, practical or artistic skills, oblige their possessors to employ them in ways that will benefit the greatest number."

—*Catechism of the Catholic Church*, 2405 (578)

"Therefore political leaders, and citizens of rich countries considered as individuals, especially if they are Christians, have the moral obligation, according to the degree of each one's responsibility, to take into consideration, in personal decisions and decisions of government, this relationship of universality, this interdependence which exists between their conduct and the poverty and underdevelopment of so many millions of people."

—St. John Paul II, *Sollicitudo rei socialis*, 9

"The obligation to commit oneself to the development of peoples is not just an individual duty, and still less an individualistic one, as if it were possible to achieve this development through the isolated efforts of each individual. It is an imperative which obliges each and every man and woman, as well as societies and nations."

—St. John Paul II, *Sollicitudo rei socialis*, 32

"When individuals and communities do not see a rigorous respect for the moral, cultural and spiritual requirements, based on the dignity of the person and on the proper identity of each community, beginning with the family and religious societies, then all the rest—availability of goods, abundance of technical resources applied to daily life, a certain level of material well-being—will prove unsatisfying and in the end contemptible."

—St. John Paul II, *Sollicitudo rei socialis*, 33

"We would also say a word to those who travel to newly industrialized nations for business purposes: industrialists, merchants, managers and representatives of large business concerns. It often happens that in their own land they do not lack a social sense. Why is it, then, that they give in to baser motives of self-interest when they set out to do business in the developing countries? Their more favored position should rather spur them on to be initiators of social progress and human betterment in these lands. Their organizational experience should help them to figure out ways to make intelligent use of the labor of the indigenous population, to develop skilled workers, to train engineers and other management men, to foster these people's initiative and prepare them for offices of ever greater responsibility. In this way they will prepare these people to take over the burden of management in the near future."

—Paul VI, *Populorum progressio*, 70

"Economic progress must be accompanied by a corresponding social progress, so that all classes of citizens can participate in the increased productivity."

—St. John XXIII, *Mater et magistra*, 73

"Justice and humanity demand that those countries which produce consumer goods, especially farm products, in excess of their own needs should come to the assistance of those other countries where large sections of the population are suffering from want and hunger. It is nothing less than an outrage to justice and humanity to destroy or to squander goods that other people need for their very lives."

—St. John XXIII, *Mater et magistra*, 161

103. May we open up a manufacturing plant in China, where our own managers will be involved in enforcing China's "one child" policy (which includes the possibility of forced abortions)?

"When immediate material cooperation concerns grave attacks on human life, it is always to be considered illicit, given the precious nature of the value in question."

—Pontifical Academy for Life, "Moral Reflections on Vaccines Prepared from Cells Derived from Aborted Human Foetuses" (June 5, 2005)

"It is very alarming to see governments in many countries launching systematic campaigns against birth, contrary not only to the cultural and religious identity of the countries themselves but also contrary to the nature of true development."

—St. John Paul II, *Sollicitudo rei socialis,* 25

104. What considerations should we address when marketing consumer goods in developing countries?

"[Advertising, used as a tool for the promotion of consumerism,] is a serious abuse, an affront to human dignity and the common good when it occurs in affluent societies. But the abuse is still more grave when consumerist attitudes and values are transmitted by communications media and advertising to developing countries, where they exacerbate socio-economic problems and harm the poor."

—Pontifical Council for Social Communications, "Ethics in Advertising," 10

"It is true that a judicious use of advertising can stimulate developing countries to improve their standard of living. But serious harm can be done them if advertising and commercial pressure become so irresponsible that communities that seek to rise from poverty to a reasonable standard of living are persuaded to seek this progress by satisfying wants that have been created artificially. The result of this is that they waste their resources and neglect their real needs and genuine development falls behind."

—*Communio et progressio,* 61

−7−

Particularly Morally
Sensitive Industries

Health Care

105. Should healthcare workers refuse to participate in actions that are intentionally harmful to innocent life?

"In the moral domain, [the International Congress of Catholic Pharmacists] is invited to address the issue of conscientious objection, which is a right your profession must recognize, permitting you not to collaborate either directly or indirectly by supplying products for the purpose of decisions that are clearly immoral such as, for example, abortion or euthanasia."

—Benedict XVI, address to members of the International Congress of Catholic Pharmacists (October 29, 2007)

"The passing of unjust laws often raises difficult problems of conscience for morally upright people with regard to the issue of cooperation, since they have a right to demand not to be forced to take part in morally evil actions. Sometimes the choices which have to be made are difficult; they may require the sacrifice of prestigious professional positions or the relinquishing of reasonable hopes of career advancement....

"To refuse to take part in committing an injustice is not only a moral duty; it is also a basic human right. Were this not so, the human person would be forced to perform an action intrinsically incompatible with human dignity, and in this way human freedom itself, the authentic meaning and purpose of which are found in its orientation to the true and the good, would be radically compromised. What is at stake therefore is an essential right which, precisely as such, should be acknowledged and protected by civil law. In this sense, the opportunity to refuse to take part in the phases of consultation, preparation and execution of these acts against life should be guaranteed to physicians, health-care personnel, and directors of hospitals, clinics and convalescent facilities. Those who have recourse to conscientious objection must be protected not only from legal penalties but also from any negative effects on the legal, disciplinary, financial and professional plane."

—St. John Paul II, *Evangelium vitae*, 74

106. Is it morally permissible to be commercially involved with experiments on embryos or fetuses?

"Medical research must refrain from operations on live embryos, unless there is a moral certainty of not causing harm to the life or integrity of the unborn child and the mother, and on condition that the parents have given their free and informed consent to the procedure. It follows that all research, even when limited to the simple observation of the embryo, would become illicit were it to involve risk to the embryo's physical integrity or life by reason of the methods used or the effects induced. As regards experimentation, and presupposing the general distinction between experimentation for purposes which are not directly therapeutic and experimentation which is clearly therapeutic for the subject himself, in the case in point one must also distinguish between experimentation carried out on embryos which are still alive and experimentation carried out on embryos which are dead. *If the embryos are living, whether viable or not, they must be respected just like any other human person; experimentation on embryos which is not directly therapeutic is illicit.* No objective, even though noble in itself, such as a foreseeable advantage to science, to other human beings or to society, can in any way justify experimentation on living human embryos or fetuses, whether viable or not, either inside or outside the mother's womb. The informed consent ordinarily required for clinical experimentation on adults cannot be granted by the parents, who may not freely dispose of the physical integrity or life of the unborn child. Moreover, experimentation on embryos and fetuses always involves risk, and indeed in most cases it involves the certain expectation of harm to their physical integrity or even their death. To use human embryos or fetuses as the object or instrument of experimentation constitutes a crime against their dignity as human beings having a right to the same respect that is due to the child already born and to every human person."

—Congregation for the Doctrine of the Faith, *Donum vitae*, 4

"The lay faithful, having responsibility in various capacities and at different levels of science as well as in the medical, social, legislative and economic fields must *courageously accept the 'challenge' posed by new problems in bioethics.* The Synod Fathers used these words: 'Christians ought to exercise their responsibilities as masters of science and technology, and not become their slaves....In view of the moral challenges presented by enormous new technological power, endangering not only fundamental human rights but the very biological essence of the human species, it is of utmost importance that lay Christians with the help of the universal Church take up the task of calling culture back to the principles of an authentic humanism, giving a dynamic and sure foundation to the promotion and defense of the rights of the human being in one's very essence, an essence which the preaching of the Gospel reveals to all.'"

—St. John Paul II, *Christifideles laici, 38*

107. Is it morally permissible to be involved with (e.g., invest in) firms that are researching various methods of genetic manipulation to produce traits in children that are considered desirable?

"*Certain attempts to influence chromosomic or genetic inheritance are not therapeutic but are aimed at producing human beings selected according to sex or other predetermined qualities. These manipulations are contrary to the personal dignity of the human being and his or her integrity and identity.* Therefore in no way can they be justified on the grounds of possible beneficial consequences for future humanity. Every person must be respected for himself: in this consists the dignity and right of every human being from his or her beginning."

—Congregation for the Doctrine of the Faith, *Donum vitae, 6*

108. Is it morally permissible to be involved with (e.g., invest in) firms that offer in vitro fertilization or artificial insemination?

"Techniques that entail the dissociation of husband and wife, by the intrusion of a person other than the couple (donation of sperm or ovum, surrogate uterus), are gravely immoral. These techniques (heterologous artificial insemination and fertilization) infringe upon a child's right to be born of a father and mother known to him and bound to each other by marriage. They betray the spouses' 'right to become a father and a mother only through each other.'"

Catechism of the Catholic Church, 2376

"Techniques involving only the married couple (homologous artificial insemination and fertilization) are perhaps less reprehensible, yet remain morally unacceptable. They dissociate the sexual act from the procreative act. The act which brings the child into existence is no longer an act by which two persons give themselves to one another, but one that 'entrusts the life and identity of the embryo into the power of doctors and biologists and establishes the domination of technology over the origin and destiny of the human person. Such a relationship of domination is in itself contrary to the dignity and equality that must be common to parents and children.' 'Under the moral aspect procreation is deprived of its proper perfection when it is not willed as the fruit of the conjugal act, that is to say, of the specific act of the spouses' union. . . . Only respect for the link between the meanings of the conjugal act and respect for the unity of the human being make possible procreation in conformity with the dignity of the person.'"

—*Catechism of the Catholic Church, 2377 (571)*

109. Is it morally permissible to be involved with (e.g., invest in) firms that offer sterilization services?

"To be condemned, as the magisterium of the Church has affirmed on many occasions, is direct sterilization, whether of the man or of the woman, whether permanent or temporary."

—Paul VI, *Humanae vitae*, 14

Pharmaceuticals

110. May we invest in bio-tech companies if part of their operations includes embryonic stem-cell research or other methods of research considered unethical by the Church?

"When the human body, considered apart from spirit and thought, comes to be used as *raw material* in the same way that the bodies of animals are used—and this actually occurs for example in experimentation on embryos and fetuses—we will inevitably arrive at a dreadful ethical defeat."

—St. John Paul II, "Letter to Families," 19

111. What are the moral responsibilities of pharmaceutical companies and pharmacists?

"The current development of an arsenal of medicines and the resulting possibilities for treatment oblige pharmacists to reflect on the ever broader functions they are called to fulfill, particularly as intermediaries between doctor and patient; they have an educational role with patients to teach the proper dosage of their medication and especially to acquaint them with the ethical implications of the use of certain drugs. In this context, it is not possible to anaesthetize consciences, for example, concerning the effects of particles whose purpose is to prevent an embryo's implantation or to shorten a person's life. The pharmacist must invite each person to advance humanity, so that every being may be protected from the moment of birth until natural death, and that medicines may fulfill properly their therapeutic role. No person, moreover, may be used thoughtlessly as an object for the purpose of therapeutic experimentation; therapeutic experimentation must take place in accordance with protocols that respect fundamental ethical norms. Every treatment or process of experimentation must be with a view to possible improvement of the person's physical condition and not merely seeking scientific advances. The pursuit of good for humanity cannot be to the detriment of people undergoing treatment. In the moral domain, your Federation is invited to address the issue of conscientious objection, which is a right your profession must recognize, permitting you not to collaborate either directly or indirectly by supplying products for the purpose of decisions that are clearly immoral such as, for example, abortion or euthanasia.

"It would also be advisable that the different pharmaceutical structures, laboratories at hospital centers and surgeries, as well as our contemporaries all together, be concerned with showing solidarity in the therapeutic context, to make access to treatment and urgently needed medicines available at all levels of society and in all countries, particularly to the poorest people.

"Prompted by the Holy Spirit, may you as Catholic pharmacists find in the life of faith and the Church's teaching elements that will guide you in your professional approach to the sick who are in need of human and moral support if they are to live with hope and find the inner resources that will help them throughout their lives. It is also your duty to help young people who enter the different pharmaceutical professions to reflect on the increasingly delicate ethical implications of their activities and decisions. To this end, it is important that all Catholic health-care professionals and people of good will join forces to deepen their formation, not only at the technical level but also with regard to bioethical issues, as well as to propose this formation to the profession as a whole. The human being, because he or she is the image or likeness of God, must always be at the center of research and choices in the biomedical context. At the same time, the natural principle of duty to provide for the care of the sick person is fundamental. The biomedical sciences are at the service of the human being; if this were not the case, they would have a cold and inhuman character. All scientific knowledge in the health sector and every therapeutic procedure is at the service of the sick person, viewed in his integral being, who must be an active partner in his treatment and whose autonomy must be respected."

—Benedict XVI, address to members of the International Congress of Catholic Pharmacists (October 29, 2007)

"Let not your keen mental powers cause you to give money undue consideration and demand the highest prices possible. We are not unaware of the astuteness, the wisdom, and the attention required for the preparation of medicines, the long hours you spend on your formulas, and the scarcity of the materials which you use. Yet, as you weigh those drops of medicine on your scales, weigh also those drops of human sweat by which men earn their bread by their hard work in mines, in quarries, in factories and elsewhere. Weigh also the tears of parents who are prepared to spend everything to snatch their dear children from the jaws of death. And finally see to it that you do not weigh out more than is necessary, just for the sake of a sale. Let not compassion be forgotten when large firms establish prices for their medicines; for as far as is in his power, man must love his fellow man. We ask your forgiveness if our words have been burdensome, but surely it is Our Apostolic duty to make constant efforts to protect and to plead the cause of the poor.

—Pius XII, discourse to participants in the International Congress of the History of Pharmacy, "Pharmacy: An Ancient and Modern Art" (September 11, 1954)

Media

112. Should we have any moral concerns about working in the media industry?

"The question of the presence of Christians in the professional world of social communications now calls for close consideration. If there is a sector of present-day life where this presence is especially necessary and desirable, it is surely that of social communications. Families should not be deterred by any misgiving they might have when one of their members wishes to embark on such a career. Evil that is much more publicized than good, is not bound up with one particular profession more than with another. Thank God, in the world of social communications, no less than in others, there are shining examples of moral living both in professional and in family life. There are those in the world of journalism, the theatre and the field of motion pictures who live out their faith in God in the calm and conscientious exercise of their profession. The very history of Christianity teaches us that the force of evangelical leaven increases rather than diminishes in proportion to the difficulties caused by one's environment. The evangelical leaven gathers force by vivifying and transforming an environment. Young people who have received a solid moral and religious formation and who are inspired by a genuine ideal are therefore, to be encouraged to engage in the different activities of social communication."

—Paul VI, message for World Social Communications Day 1969

113. What are the responsibilities of those who work in the media?

"Christian communicators need a formation which enables them to work effectively in a media environment of this kind. Such a formation will have to be comprehensive: training in technical skills; training in ethics and morality, with particular attention to values and norms relevant to their professional work; training in human culture, in philosophy, history, social sciences and aesthetics. But, before all else, it will have to be a formation in the interior life, the life of the spirit.

"Christian communicators need to be men and women of Spirit-filled prayer, entering ever more deeply into communion with God in order to grow in their ability to foster communion among their fellow human beings. They must be schooled in hope by the Holy Spirit, 'the principal agent of the new evangelization' (*Tertio Millennio Adveniente,* 45), so that they can communicate hope to others."

—St. John Paul II, message for World Communications Day 1998

"In fulfilling its public responsibilities, the television industry should develop and observe a code of ethics which includes

a commitment to serving the needs of families and to promoting values supportive of family life. Media councils, with
members from both the industry and the general public, are
also a highly desirable way of making television more responsive to the needs and values of its audiences."

—St. John Paul II, message for World Communications Day 1994

"The professional who rates at its true value the impact and influence of the media productions he creates, will take particular care to make them of such high moral quality that their
effect upon the formation of the culture of his generation, will
be invariably a positive one. To be true to himself, to his craft,
and to his faith, he must evidently resist the ever-present blan-
dishments of easy profit, and firmly refuse to take part in any
production which exploits human weakness, offends human
conscience, or affronts human dignity."

—St. John Paul II, message for World Communications Day 1993

"But what we are asking for today is positive action on the part
of all Catholics and especially those engaged in the mass media, to diffuse in all their fullness the values of Christ's life-giving message and to make the world ring with their conviction,
with the voice of their belief and with the Word of God. This is
indeed an important vocation and a great service to the world.
And we appeal likewise for a full measure of partnership with
all brother Christians and with all men of good will in every
land to affirm effectively the common principles upon which
the dignity of man depends. We are asking all those engaged
in social communications to tell the story of the sacrifice and
dedication that exists in the world, to make known the good
that abounds, and the dynamism, enthusiasm and selflessness
of so many, especially among the young. We know that there

are numerous 'Media Men' of good will who burn with the desire and determination to turn their 'lifeless instruments' to the benefit of their fellowmen. We ask them all to renew their resolve to transform the mass media into burning torches and powerful beacons illuminating the path to the only true happiness. The world needs the affirmation of spiritual values as seen in their concrete expression. To reach this goal those who are able to use social communications in all their expressions must do so. The language of image and print, of light, music and sound must help to convey the message of goodness, beauty and truth. The press, the radio, television, the cinema, the theater and advertising must be utilized to the full in this mission of conveying a meaningful message to the world."

—Paul VI, message for World Social Communications Day 1973

"Those whose job it is to give news have a most difficult and responsible role to play. They face formidable obstacles and these obstacles will sometimes include persons interested in concealing the truth. This is especially the case for reporters who give close-up impressions of the news and who, in order to do this, often travel to the four corners of the earth in order to witness events as they actually happen. At times they risk their lives and indeed a number of them have been killed in this line of duty. The safety of such correspondents should be ensured in every possible way because of the service they render to man's right to know about what is happening. This is particularly true in the case of wars which involve and concern the whole human race. So the Church utterly condemns the use of violence against newsmen or against anyone in any way involved in the passing on of news. For these persons vindicate and practice the right of finding out what is happening and of passing on this information to others.

"It is hard for anyone to learn the whole truth and to pass this on to others, but newsmen face an additional problem. Of its nature, news is about what is new. So journalists deal with what has just happened and with what is of present interest. More than that, out of a mass of material, they must select what they judge to be the significant facts that will concern their audience. So it can happen that the news reported is only a part of the whole and does not convey what is of real importance.

"Communicators must give news that is quick, complete and comprehensible. So more and more they have to seek out competent men for comments, background briefing and discussion. Often these comments are required immediately, sometimes even before the expected event has happened. Men of trust, especially when they are in a position of responsibility or authority, are rightly reluctant to make hasty or unprepared comments before they have had a chance to study a situation and its context. And so because the media are impelled to demand quick comment, the initiative often passes to men who are less responsible and less well-informed but who are more willing to oblige. Those acquainted with a given situation should try to prevent this happening. As far as they can, they should keep themselves up to date so that they themselves can reply and ensure that the public is properly informed.

"Then there is another problem. Those who have to keep the public informed must give the news quickly if it is to appear fresh and interesting. Competition also obliges them to do this and speed is often won at the price of accuracy. The communicator has also to know the tastes and cultural level of his public and to take into account its known preferences. And when he comes to present the news, it is in the face of such hazards that a communicator must remain faithful to the truth.

"But as well as these problems which are inherent in the nature of the news and communications media, there is another. Communicators must hold the wandering attention of a harried and hurried public by vivid reporting. And yet they must not give way to the temptation of making the news sensational in such a way that they risk distorting it by taking it out of context or by exaggerating it out of all proportion.

"The recipients who piece together the news that comes to them in fragments may well end up with an unbalanced or distorted idea of the whole picture. To a certain extent, accuracy can be restored by the continuity of the flow from different sources, which must always be carefully assessed. The recipients of information should have a clear conception of the predicament of those that purvey information. They should not look for a superhuman perfection in the communicators. What they do have a right and duty to expect, however, is that a rapid and clear correction should follow any mistake or misrepresentation that has found its way into a report. They are to protest whenever omissions or distortions occur. They are to protest whenever events have been reported out of context or in a biased manner. They are to protest whenever the significance of events has been wildly exaggerated or underplayed. This right should be guaranteed for recipients by agreement among the communicators themselves and, if this cannot be got, then by national law or international convention."

—Pastoral Instruction *Communio et progressio*, 37–41 1971

"The media of social communication do more than present the traditional forms of artistic expression; they themselves create new ones. And now that the media cover the whole earth and multiply the opportunities for international cultural cooperation, especially in co-productions using the talents of artists from many nations, it is only right that both communicators and recipients should seek to acquire a truly catholic taste, one that includes both the traditional and the latest forms of artistic expression, one that appreciates and understands the production of all nations, of all cultures and of all sub-cultures within the same areas of civilization."

—*Communio et progressio*, 54

"Because factual information provides a public service, not only must news reporting keep to the facts, and bear down upon the most important of these but the meaning of what it reports should be brought out by explanation. The real bearing of one item of news upon another should be pointed out especially when different items reach the recipient without evidence of any discernible pattern. In this way the recipient will be able to use this information as a basis for his judgement and decision in matters affecting the community."

—*Communio et progressio*, 75

"The principal moral responsibility for the proper use of the media of social communication falls on newsmen, writers, actors, designers, producers, displayers, distributors, operators and sellers, as well as critics and all others who play any part in the production and transmission of mass presentations. It is quite evident what gravely important responsibilities they have in the present day when they are in a position to lead the human race to good or to evil by informing or arousing mankind.

"Thus, they must adjust their economic, political or artistic and technical aspects so as never to oppose the common good. For the purpose of better achieving this goal, they are to be commended when they join professional associations, which—even under a code, if necessary, of sound moral practice—oblige their members to show respect for morality in the duties and tasks of their craft."

—Paul VI *Inter mirifica*, 11 1963

114. In news media or advertisements may we present facts in such a way as to favor one view or product over another?

"Objectivity in information is something essential and irreplaceable, for each one of us requires to know the truth, in order that he may develop his personality fully according to its yardstick, as well as exercising his social responsibilities on the basis of reliable information. This is our right, and its proper exercise presupposes that facts have been honestly reported. All the better if the bare presentation of the facts is supported with well-informed comment, for this, by placing the facts in the full context in which they occur and by showing what relationship they have to human values, makes it easier to understand their meaning.

"But quite evidently, such upright and honorable methods, employed sincerely for the purpose of setting the truth in relief and making it comprehensible, are not to be confused with those processes and techniques which, under the pretense of 'neutrality' and 'independence,' actually set themselves to manipulate the facts and thereby to manipulate also the audiences to which they are presented. For practices of this nature there can be no commendation."

—Paul VI, message for World Communications Day 1975

115. Are there any particular topics that we should be especially sensitive to when working in the media?

"The family and family life are all too often inadequately portrayed in the media. Infidelity, sexual activity outside of marriage, and the absence of a moral and spiritual vision of the marriage covenant are depicted uncritically, while positive support is at times given to divorce, contraception, abortion and homosexuality. Such portrayals, by promoting causes inimical to marriage and the family, are detrimental to the common good of society."

—St. John Paul II, message for World Communications Day 2004

— 8 —

Conclusion

116. Are there any general themes that seem to occur throughout Church teaching about the responsibilities of Christians in business?

"Love, overflowing with small gestures of mutual care, is also civic and political, and it makes itself felt in every action that seeks to build a better world. Love for society and commitment to the common good are outstanding expressions of a charity which affects not only relationships between individuals but also 'macro-relationships, social, economic and political ones.' That is why the Church set before the world the ideal of a 'civilization of love.' Social love is the key to authentic development: 'In order to make society more human, more worthy of the human person, love in social life—political, economic and cultural—must be given renewed value, becoming the constant and highest norm for all activity.'"

—Francis, Laudato Si, 231 (quoting Benedict XVI, *Caritas in Veritate*, 2; Paul VI, *Message for the 1977 World Day of Peace*; Pontifical Council for Justice and Peace, *Compendium of the Social Doctrine of the Church*, 582.

"Even in the most difficult and complex times, besides recognizing what is happening, we must above all else turn to God's love."

—Benedict XVI, *Caritas in veritate*, 79

"The Church's social doctrine holds that authentically human social relationships of friendship, solidarity and reciprocity can also be conducted within economic activity, and not only outside it or 'after' it. The economic sphere is neither ethically neutral, nor inherently inhuman and opposed to society. It is part and parcel of human activity and precisely because it is human, it must be structured and governed in an ethical manner."

—Benedict XVI, *Caritas in veritate*, 36

"It is not the elemental spirits of the universe, the laws of matter, which ultimately govern the world and mankind, but a personal God governs the stars, that is, the universe; it is not the laws of matter and of evolution that have the final say, but reason, will, love—a Person. And if we know this Person and he knows us, then truly the inexorable power of material elements no longer has the last word; we are not slaves of the universe and of its laws, we are free. In ancient times, honest enquiring minds were aware of this. Heaven is not empty. Life is not a simple product of laws and the randomness of matter, but within everything and at the same time above everything, there is a personal will, there is a Spirit who in Jesus has revealed himself as Love."

—Benedict XVI, *Spe salvi*, 5

"The purpose of a business firm is not simply to make a profit, but is to be found in its very existence as a *community of per-*

sons who in various ways are endeavoring to satisfy their basic needs, and who form a particular group at the service of the whole of society."

—St. John Paul II, *Centesimus annus*, 35

"What are less than human conditions? The material poverty of those who lack the bare necessities of life, and the moral poverty of those who are crushed under the weight of their own self-love; oppressive political structures resulting from the abuse of ownership or the improper exercise of power, from the exploitation of the worker or unjust transactions.

"What are truly human conditions? The rise from poverty to the acquisition of life's necessities; the elimination of social ills; broadening the horizons of knowledge; acquiring refinement and culture. From there one can go on to acquire a growing awareness of other people's dignity, a taste for the spirit of poverty, an active interest in the common good, and a desire for peace. Then man can acknowledge the highest values and God Himself, their author and end. Finally and above all, there is faith—God's gift to men of good will—and our loving unity in Christ, who calls all men to share God's life as sons of the living God, the Father of all men."

—Paul VI, *Populorum progressio*, 21

"The great truth which we learn from nature herself is also the grand Christian dogma on which religion rests as on its foundation—that, when we have given up this present life, then shall we really begin to live. God has not created us for the perishable and transitory things of earth, but for things heavenly and everlasting; He has given us this world as a place of exile, and not as our abiding place. As for riches and the other things which men call good and desirable, whether we have them in abundance, or are lacking in them—so far as eternal happiness is concerned—it makes no difference; the only important thing is to use them aright. Jesus Christ, when He redeemed us with plentiful redemption, took not away the pains and sorrows which in such large proportion are woven together in the web of our mortal life. He transformed them into motives of virtue and occasions of merit; and no man can hope for eternal reward unless he follow in the blood-stained footprints of his Savior. 'If we suffer with Him, we shall also reign with Him' (2 Tm 2:12). Christ's labors and sufferings, accepted of His own free will, have marvelously sweetened all suffering and all labor. And not only by His example, but by His grace and by the hope held forth of everlasting recompense, has He made pain and grief more easy to endure; 'for that which is at present momentary and light of our tribulation, worketh for us above measure exceedingly an eternal weight of glory' (2 Cor 4:17).

"Therefore, those whom fortune favors are warned that riches do not bring freedom from sorrow and are of no avail for eternal happiness, but rather are obstacles (Mt 19:23–24); that the rich should tremble at the threatenings of Jesus Christ—threatenings so unwonted in the mouth of our Lord (Lk 6:24–25)—and that a most strict account must be given to the Supreme Judge for all we possess."

—Leo XIII, *Rerum novarum*, 21–22

Index